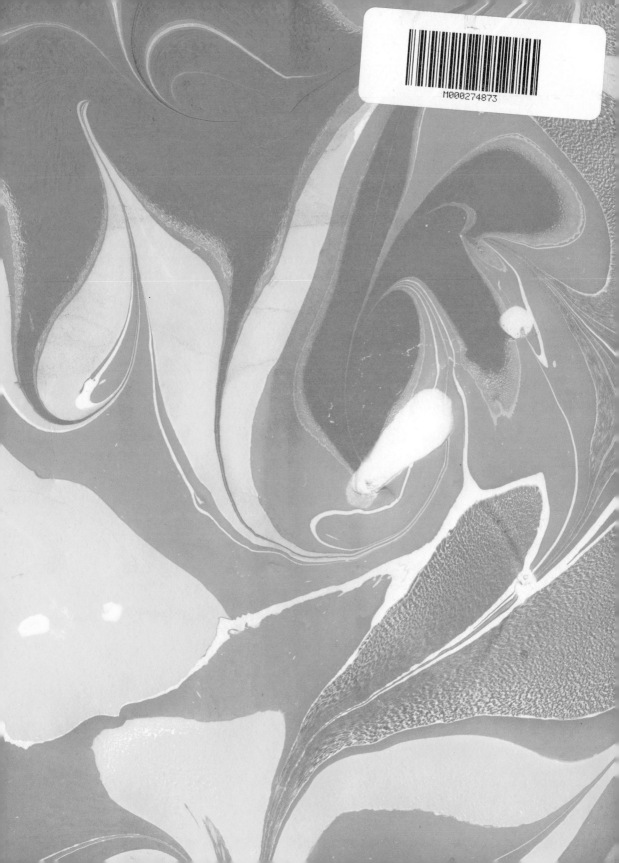

THE BIG REVEAL

HARPER

An Imprint of HarperCollins*Publishers*

THE BIG REVEAL

an illustrated
manifesto
of drag

SASHA VELOUR

HarperCollins books may be purchased for educational, business, or sales promotional use. For information, please email the Special Markets Department at SPsales@harpercollins.com.

FIRST EDITION

All images are from the House of Velour unless otherwise noted.

An extension of this copyright appears on page 204.

Designed by Sasha Velour and Nancy Singer

Library of Congress Cataloging-in-Publication Data has been applied for.

ISBN 978–0–35–850808–3

23 24 25 26 27   TC   10 9 8 7 6 5 4 3 2 1

For you, my family —
quilted together across
dimensions and times —
who taught me how to tell
My STORY and keep SURVIVING.
I love you ♡

Contents

ABOUT THE AUTHOR

SASHA VELOUR is a gender-fluid drag queen, artist, and speaker. She is the creator and editor of the critically acclaimed drag magazine *Velour* and the host of the influential New York City drag show *NightGowns*, which was adapted into a docuseries. Her first one-queen theater show, *Smoke & Mirrors*, toured to sold-out audiences around the world. In 2017 she was crowned the winner of *RuPaul's Drag Race* Season 9 on VH1, with an emotional and reveal-filled finale performance that made history. Velour also holds a degree in literature from Vassar College, an MFA in cartooning from the Center for Cartoon Studies, and was a former Fulbright Scholar in Moscow. This is her first book.

SASHA DE LOUR

PUT ON SOME CLOTHES!!

reveal   was d
was extremely sim
ith all things, the de
ith the cleanly trimm
had an expert se
ssing room, the
the season c
me upside d
re diving in
earlier, I discovere
d to lift the wig slow

se petal
mit that it w
But as with a
l stiff, with the
finale we had
d in the dressing
all of us i
red wig fo
a bowl ro
iced earlier,
had to lift the w
uld be racing
as well put it t
ed all the poss
ny carpeted sp
hone in a wate
ck into a Zip
—a drag king
tuff more in
y slid fists of
enough?" He a
r stuff more in!!!"
oly had more than e
t from beneath the
ut while I took deep b
nd I stood backstage
wall, displaying every c
show's new "lipsync for the

♡ DO YOUR BEST... ♔ OR ELSE

I did actually have a secret, but it wasn't sexy. That morning, I
load of my feats worked on my phone and discovered that my
credit cards were a hundred thousand dollars in the red and
counting. My motel projects had tumbled into the red and
disaster. My most projects had pool on a month, and my price
closed from Drag manager was most a cost of nightmare and I
needed me from cheap pay on more stage videos for me—
the theater months, but as my mismanage anker was making
The job itself was smooth, but on our right track, I mounted
reassuring me with making it all as mouth prominent and
announcing that all stars would be new on right next, I pranced
out into the darkness while propping in an almost bulking my
whole, the others, without blanket from used across—
Hey... I said to myself—come up to the stage,
star I felt, almost ahead, another moment of my exciting
before I was in another, cold and passionate hugs. As the
announcing or been encouraging or
either, I asked to wander across the world of drag a dined
out as an sexy of modifying, I began how to ground a
reduction all become, come on home. It been so off
allowing all for at, but I still held fast and tried to make the most of
it.

Before I can even talk about making
of some of my worst failures
had Nina Simone's "Break Down and Let
and just screamed in the audience's
then my pink plastic heel broke off. I
well, that worked in my head." I
even though I wish it wasn't.

I directed and hosted the brand
final, Baz Luhrmann, Whoopi
sweaty. I'm afraid I'm among
maybe in history. It's a big
adapted on the sweatiest
e-pads under sensitive
my entire torso in saran
I dropped the
ped my front tooth
natically after my
th, and could feel a

as the time I

house. In a
—on
They
atched.
hat we

TA
MM
DA!

WIDE
AWAKE!

Bars,
Balls, Bathhouses
for cottages
DRAG
Molly
houses,
POLARI,
Tranny
SHAMMY
SPIRITUAL
TRANSFORMERS
MAMA
CHURCH
ROMAN

Ritual

Drag is everywhere. There isn't a corner of the world that hasn't seen a little drag at some point—a wig, a frock, a dance, a swish. Sure, you might have to dig around some fragmented sources and do a little reading past the euphemisms, exclusions, and whitewashings of history to clearly see it, but the truth is . . . there have always been shows like this.

on the roof !!

The roots of the art of drag are more ancient than the word *drag* itself. After all, identities like "queer," "trans," "cis," "gay," "straight" are modern, and the boundaries between them have changed so much that it can be tricky for any of us to trace connections to the past. The ideas of "man," "woman," or "nonbinary" are fluid, too, and mean something different to every person (as well they should). It would almost be easier to find commonality in the ways people have transgressed and subverted the expectations of gender than in the ways people have embodied them. Drag could be one such universal thread—an enduring act of transformation that cuts across boundaries of gender and culture. Drag isn't limited to who we are or where we come from . . . it cares about what we create, how we fantasize, and what we reveal to the world.

Of course, most of us who create drag are gay, lesbian, nonbinary, or trans in some way. It is the queer community who has fought the hardest to protect this art. But one of the reasons drag is so vital to us is because it opens up possibilities beyond our identities: it expands our range of expression and questions what it means for anyone to really "have" gender, sexual identity, attraction, or repulsion to begin with. The enduring conclusion: Our bodies, our sexes, our outfits, our choices. Drag is a queer and feminist project because it demands freedom of choice for all, and reimagines gender into something that could no longer hold power over anyone. A society that fully accepts drag as a natural part of human

Voilà !

expression might finally be ready to make room for queer and trans people to exist in real life, not just onstage. Perhaps that day is not so far off.

I swear this isn't just me trying to make myself feel important as a drag queen . . . Although that's definitely part of the gig—we declare our own value in a world that doesn't necessarily want us in order to survive against all odds (hence the "queen" of it all). But the fact is, people have always loved drag. If there is anything at all "essential" in the human spirit, it might just be the way we love dressing up and becoming someone else—beyond all limitations of gender or status, beyond any expectations of respectability or reality. Just as importantly (or even more so), it seems that people also love to cheer these displays on. Some say you haven't lived until you've watched a drag show, taking part in the collective reimagining that our performances inevitably inspire (or demand). I often think the real magic of drag is the way the audience reveals itself in turn.

These traditions go way back. Some of the earliest hints of what we call "drag" lie in Mesolithic-age rituals from Central Asia and Siberia. More than fifteen thousand years ago, spiritual healers, sometimes called shamans, transformed their genders to dance for good luck, in commemoration of the dead, at yearly festivals, and more. They appeared in embellished costumes and performed with smoke, fire, and shadows to a drumbeat. It took only a simple gesture to signify a change, like putting their hair into a long braid to channel the feminine. Sometimes they transformed beyond the limits of reality entirely—becoming genderless spirits or dead ancestors. The word *shaman* comes from a Tungusic language and is often translated as "one who knows" because their rituals were designed to impart truths about the past, the present, and the future.

Just like at any drag show, audiences left with new awareness and intention for their lives. Inside and outside of the rituals, they saw shamans as a third kind of gender—neither "man" or "woman" but somehow beyond, connected

Buryat Shaman

to the spiritual realm, infused with magical powers, and touched by the divine (usually feminine). Biology was rarely a factor in who could become a shaman. Instead . . . this was about a calling from the universe!

Similar types of figures existed all over the world, but the only people who really called themselves shamans were the spiritual guides of the aforementioned Tungusic societies. In the eighteenth century, as empires spread, Western European scholars appropriated this term for all kinds of Indigenous healers, especially those who employed gender transformations and drag.

The word *shaman* was used to describe the *lhamana* among the Zuni people in what is now southwestern United States, the *machi* of the Mapuche in what is now Argentina and Chile, the *isangoma* in Zulu South Africa, and many others, obliterating their unique names, and their different philosophies of gender, expression, and spirituality.

Although these may all be examples of early queer expression, the concept of grouping them together carries the weight of historical violence and erasure. It was European anthropologists who really shaped the modern idea of shamans when they flooded journals with "shocking" stories of costumes made of mirrors, bones, and feathers, drum rituals, and outlandish drag dances.

These same writers began to link the word *shaman* to shams and scams, labeling ritual dancers as witches and con artists. This was another way for Europeans to discredit Indigenous ways of life, and they decried the widespread tolerance for gender nonconforming people as "devilish" or "unnatural."

The histories of queerness, transness, and drag are difficult to unentangle—and they've become extra muddled due to this history of colonial conflations. As a result, we are not all in agreement about how to draw connections, or which legacies to claim as our own. Suffice it to say: many Indigenous cultures around the world turned to drag, performative gender

We'wha, a Lhamana

Mapuche Machi →

transformation, as a spiritual and creative practice, while at the same time accommodating genders and sexes outside of a strict binary in everyday life.

In the revolutionary 1992 pamphlet *Transgender Liberation*, Leslie Feinberg argues that queer and trans expression was eradicated under the changing worldview spread by imperialism and early capitalism, which elevated Eurocentric cultural norms above all others. Women, femininity, queerness, and non-whiteness all came to be seen as inferior to white masculinity in an attempt to establish and retain power for the men who were literally writing the rules.

As global empire and Christianity spread at the beginning of the first millennium, so did the first institutionalized fears around drag and queerness. Christian conferences such as the First Council of Nicaea in 325 and the Code of Justinian in the sixth century were among the first to explicitly ban gender-fluid rituals and mystery cults (ostensibly as part of the persecution of paganism at large). Their soldiers cracked down on the Thracian *baptai*, a draggy mystery cult whose devotees officiated in long blond horse-hair wigs to serve the goddess Kotys. They also banned the *galli*, who performed castration and other body modification to worship Cybele, the great mother. They outlawed the Scythian *enarei*, priests who took on female names, smoked cannabis, and uttered prophesies in high-pitched voices. And the early church even destroyed Greek temples to Dionysus—a once-beloved nonbinary agent of chaos celebrated with a lot of drunkenness and drag.

Christianity has played a major role in the development of shame, stigma, and the criminalization of queerness worldwide. In the 1500s in West Africa, Yorubans who worshipped the nonbinary god Shango were found guilty of "witchcraft" and "sodomy" by the Portuguese inquisition and exiled to Brazil and the Caribbean. In their new homes, some revived their Yoruban traditions in the form of hybrid religions like Santería and Condomblé, which include queer offshoots to this day. In China, the Jesuit missionary Matteo Ricci first brought Christian moral panic to Beijing in 1610, warning that the rouged and costumed "boys who play music, sing and dance" are "the most vicious people

TRANS GENDER LIBERATION
A movement whose time has come
By Leslie Feinberg

by Leslie Feinberg

4

of the whole country." Likewise, Protestant British officials in India during the 1800s described the Kinnar (or Hijra), a deeply rooted part of Hindu tradition, as "agents of contagion and a source of moral danger."

People grew to be afraid of all kinds of queer expression, without any distinctions between them. Their fears were used as a moral justification for killing people, destroying their cultures, and stealing their land and resources. In North and South America, colonizers used the word *berdache* (from a French gay slang word meaning "bottom") to describe all nonconforming people they saw, and frequently murdered. This derogatory word was used for queer Indigenous Americans for centuries, even within the communities themselves (after the languages of colonization were forced on them). In 1990, *berdache* was replaced with the term "two-spirit," a decision made by an Indigenous LGBTQ gathering in Winnipeg, Manitoba. But even with positive intention, the concept of a single term carries the weight of much pain and loss. From the Ojibwe *ikwekaazo* and *ininiikaazo* to the Lakota *winkte*, every community and culture had their own words for queer and trans people, their own unique expressions and traditions.

Make no mistake, queer and trans people may not all identify the same way, but we do share the same mission: to fight back and survive! One legend involves Spanish explorer Francisco de Orellana, who was exploring the rainforest among the Tupinambá people of Brazil in 1542 when his boat was attacked by a tribe of transmasculine warriors. Poetically, he declared the river's new name to be the "River of the Amazons," in reference to the ancient Greek myth of warriors who cut off their breasts (his only reference for trans or nonconforming people). As it turns out, the Amazons were real: a society of transmasculine Scythians—*hamazon* meant "warrior" or "fighting together"—who defended themselves in "warrior drag" against the advancing Greek Empire. Today we still call Orellana's river the "Amazon"—a symbol of one European man's ignorance, and of queer and trans people's continued resistance. We are connected across the world in spite of constant erasure and misidentification, and partly because of it, too.

The best records that people like us existed throughout history are too often found in accounts of how we were excluded, punished, and killed. We have to read between the lines to learn how we lived, loved, and what language we used for ourselves. But with some digging, we can always find proof that we were there, and take part in the ritual of passing our stories on.

With this lack of documentation and consistent terminology, there are bound to be disagreements about what the earliest forms of queer expression really were and who has a right to claim them today. I'm sure there are some who would complain about me connecting shamanism to drag like I've just been doing. Indeed, modern uses of the word *shaman* to describe fantasies of ancestral culture are so overdone these days. In my defense, though, I'm just carrying on the grand tradition of RuPaul, Leslie Feinberg, and Kate Bornstein (who all claimed this connection)! Plus, I'm confident our claim is preferable to that of alt-right nationalists—with their neo-pagan "shamans"—who write historically inaccurate fantasies of Viking patriarchies taking over the world or of a mythic time when there were only two genders. Queer myths and oversimplifications can be dangerous in their own ways, but at least they are grounded in the truth.

We can never really know how these early performers saw their genders. But we can say they were doing a type of drag. Let's call *drag* the transformation and transcendence of gender and spirit through costume, gesture, and illusion. Whatever the context, it is clear: drag is natural, it's human, and it's always been a part of culture.

In an ideal world, of course, queer, trans, and nonbinary people wouldn't have to perform in order to survive. But we do what we have to (and a few of us really love it!). Sometimes the only ways that those of us who refuse the binaries and templates of our times can be understood is within the role of a performer—as goddess, witch, entertainer, or muse. Perhaps this is because our expressions of self seem extraordinary and unintelligible in time periods so strictly defined by binary sex and gender. Perhaps it is just the stereotype that queer people are "naturally" theatrical, performative, and unnatural. Perhaps it is because we really are touched by the divine.

Regardless, the ways we dream and talk and play are natural, onstage or off. The historical existence of queer people proves that the concept of "normal" can be (and already has been) more expansive than what any person can know. Drag reveals that who we "really are" and how people see us aren't fixed realities; they can be changed . . . perhaps just for a night, the length of a song, or even forever. Through constant transformations and reveals, drag embodies the queer possibility that exists within each of us—the infinite ways in which gender, reality, good taste, and art can be lived. At its best, drag also blurs the fragile boundary between the individual and the communal, revealing the interconnectedness of all life and thought.

My grandmas taught me everything—in fact, it was my grandma Dina who first put me in drag. Dina was born in Manchuria. Her family were Yiddish-speaking Jews who escaped antisemitic pogroms in Ukraine and helped build a multiethnic community in the city of Harbin in the 1920s. When she was little, her family went to see a shaman once while on vacation in the mountains of Mongolia. She couldn't remember what they said, but she never forgot their robes. Later, during World War II, her family was uprooted once again in order to escape the Japanese invasions. Dina told a story about the time she was trapped under dead bodies and rubble in the streets as a baby—luckily she didn't scream or else she would have been bayonetted by soldiers. Her mother, Goldie, eventually found her and pulled her free. They used

my grandparents

7

family connections in America to sail (in the belly of a cargo ship) to San Francisco, where Dina lived for the rest of her life.

Dina believed dramatic life experiences made you more theatrical, and used that excuse to explain her extravagant wardrobe, her charmingly nosy personality, and why it took her so long to set her hair and makeup every morning. As a young immigrant freshly arrived in San Francisco, she dreamed of being an actress, but as she tells it, she was always too nervous to give a good audition. Dina was criticized by casting directors for her accent, her looks, and "having no talent." But she never let that stop her from encouraging anyone else from getting into showbiz!

In the 1960s, Dina would leave my dad to babysit his sister Deborah and brother Steve at home in suburban Daly City, and drive into San Francisco with her girlfriends and their husbands to go see drag shows at Finocchio's, the world-famous cabaret of "impersonators." She would drink her favorite cocktail (Kahlua and cream) and dance on the tables, which she always swore the queens loved.

When I visited her house as a little kid, she would always encourage me to channel my inner diva. Beating out a drum rhythm on the arm of the couch, she would coach me to walk dramatically into the room, drop my coat, and reveal the look. "Fabulous!" she'd whisper knowingly. Sometimes she'd put me in a "sorceress shaman" robe and head wrap, other times it was her red swim cap, sequined cardigan, and handbag to transform into "babushka on vacation."

We'd look into the mirrored doors of her closet and admire our handiwork. On the best days, she'd dress up, too, donning

My grandma Dina

Finocchio's Program, 1950

I don't remember ever not doing DRAG...

me and grandma Dina, 1995 →

8

matching attire for synchronized swimming in the condominium pool. Papa Norman would usually indulge in being our photographer, but he was also sure to warn me: "You can't always get what you want."

I found ways to practice my rituals in secret. After I was supposed to be asleep, I would wrap myself in an old bed quilt and twirl back and forth in front of the mirror on my door, straining my vision to see in the dark. Before I knew what any of it could be called—theater, drag, queerness, glorious faggotry—I dreamed of being a performer who dressed up as a lady and put on shows for rapt audiences. At the time, I didn't think it would ever be possible. And worse, I was starting to feel shame for wanting it.

I didn't learn the word *drag* until my mom's mom, Josephine Taylor Hedges (or Grandma Jo), explained it to me. She fancied herself "the internet before it existed," having worked her entire life as a reference librarian. Jo was born into a Scottish Protestant family in Michigan in 1911. I remember that she smelled like cigarettes, drank scotch over crushed ice, collected owl figurines, loved murder mysteries, and utilized signature catchphrases like "forward the light brigade," "catty-whompus," or "I've reached my sanctifanct." She enjoyed speaking in her own folksy code, which prepared me to feel at home in the way queer people adopt our own extravagant speech patterns.

While stationed in Hawaii during World War II, Jo and Grandpa Howard enjoyed amateur drag by soldiers who staged performances and contests on the US Navy base— sometimes bawdy, other times empowering, sometimes even with feminist subplots. They were called "girlie shows" and a few of the performers grew so popular that they became near-celebrities, touring bases around the world. Imagine these

"fabulous"

at grandma Dina's

my grandma Jo

me as Cinderella, 1990

Clyde in "drag" at Rembrandt

soldiers in skirts having to pause their act to arm cannons! I prefer my shows without the war, but it still was a kind of drag.

So there we were: Grandma Jo gleefully showing me a yellowing early-1980s photo of her older brother Clyde in a flat wig, lumpy bra, and a sparse pink dress. "He's in 'drag!' You know 'drag'—it's when a fellow dresses like a lady, or a broad puts on a mustache!"

She and I both knew how well acquainted I was with the concept, but I just nodded seriously, taking it all in. Somehow it was both reassuring and upsetting to learn that there was a name for this thing I loved . . . and that it could look so very busted from the outside. Obviously, there was a lot left to learn.

from
grandma Jo's
photo album,
← 1981

At first I had so many misconceptions. I believed drag was something artificial or insincere, perhaps making fun of or parodying gender by reducing it to a few clichés. Now I know that it's not that drag artists don't take gender seriously—we take it as seriously as everyone else. It's our *selves* we refuse to take seriously—we can't afford to. Drag humor is never mean-spirited, it's a coping mechanism. What if someone calls us tragic? We respond: "Of course I'm tragic, we all are. But I tell myself I'm beautiful and that's what matters." If we can't learn to laugh at ourselves, then it would hurt too much when others did, and meant it. Only by acting a little ridiculous can we embrace the true ridiculousness of life.

From its earliest forms, drag has been a mirror that reflects, and attempts to expand, our culture's views of gender, beauty, and of queer and trans people. Today we've come to understand that "binary sex," supposedly determined by a combination of visible organs, genetics, hormones, and so on, isn't as solid as people might have thought. Most people, queer or not, fall somewhere along a spectrum of differences, and we all have to make changes to our bodies if we want to conform to binary distinctions—hair removal, working out, plastic surgery, hormone replacement, makeup, among others.

That's why drag could never be about a single transformation that transgresses the binary. There's no such thing! It's way too reductive to define drag as "men dressed as women," or "women dressed as men," although that might seem like the most obvious way to put it. In truth, drag performers often don't start out in a straightforward place when it comes to our gender, and we usually don't end in one, either.

Another of the most persistent misconceptions about drag is that it's only gay men who do it. If anything, drag invented modern gay expression, not the other way around. People developed drag routines long before words for "sexual orientation" like *gay* or *lesbian* had ever been defined; it was in drag parties and clubs that the community started to see the need for such terms to begin with. Even from my very first experiences doing drag at the club, some of the most creative drag artists I've met do *not* identify as cisgender gay men. What makes a good drag artist is the extent of your ambition to stylize these boundaries, not your adherence to one in particular.

One of the most compelling notions of drag is the idea that no one is inherently superior because of their gender or "natural" appearance. Drag can look like almost anything. It's not really about becoming something opposite to yourself, but rather revealing a heightened and transformed version that was there all along. It's not the makeup, the wig, the clothes, or the shoes that make drag. It's the conjuring of a space where adherence to gender and cultural norms isn't important. Drag is the art of bringing queer possibility to life.

But the thing that makes drag powerful is the same thing that has made it so threatening. The idea that all expressions of gender could be worthy and useful—even the seemingly bizarre or "failed" ones—continues to upset hierarchies. As with all things, the people obsessed with boundaries are the ones who are afraid they need them to stay relevant.

"Gender is a construct, tear it apart!" and all that . . . But even with the prevalence of drag and queer activism, gender remains very real and sensitive for people. Ah, well. It really doesn't matter if gender is constructed or if the binary of sex is a sham. Queer and trans people deserve to be treated as human whether you agree with their identity or not. We deserve equal rights and opportunities, no matter what anyone says.

Not so long ago the official words in English to describe us were "unnatural" or "pathic." The goal behind the adoption of words like *homosexual* or *trans* was to replace pejorative language with neutral terminology. To smash the stigmas, we've had to continue creating and revising our own lexicons for ourselves.

Words for identity are necessary, but we've had to create a wide spectrum of them to fully understand ourselves. Some words describe our unique experiences—the contexts we were raised in, the choices we have made, the things that set us apart. Other words draw us into a wider community with others—a community we choose strategically. For me, the word *drag* does both.

The word *drag* itself has a muddled history. Some claim it's an abbreviation, written into Shakespearean stage directions to mean "dressed resembling a girl." That's what RuPaul once said on *Drag Race*, even though no such thing exists (sorry, Mama!). I've also heard that *drag* comes from the German word *tragen*, meaning "to wear" or "to dress up."

The truth is . . . no one really knows! The most believable origin story, and the queerest, is that the word *drag* emerged from a language called Polari—a semisecret code used by gay people, convicts, and traveling entertainers of the nineteenth century. Because queerness was criminalized, our community had to build culture in marginalized spaces with what we had—developing a language made up of a little Yiddish, Italian, French, and a lot of working-class English slang.

Some believe the expression "putting on the drag" came to Polari from coach-driver slang for pulling the brakes on a carriage. Queer folks, ever the poetically inclined, adopted it as a metaphor for "slowing themselves down with heavy gowns." Our queer and trans pioneers faced extreme assaults from the police but they still transformed the bars and clubs where they gathered into vibrant community spaces—radical escapes where they could talk openly, perform in "drag," have sex, and develop a separate culture from the oppressive mainstream.

In England these spaces were called "Molly Houses," after a Polari nickname for both gay men and trans women. These spaces drew "mollies and their friends" together and helped generations of queer people feel a sense of kinship and normalcy. As early as 1749, a reporter wrote that "Master molly has nothing to do but slip on his Head Cloaths [a wig] and he is an errant woman." Ivan Bloch described a house in 1785 where men were "caught in the act of nursing some of their suffering 'sisters' lying in 'childbed'"—drag queens helping each other pretend to give birth to baby dolls. Without a doubt, these were shows!

In New York, similar spaces popped up throughout the 1800s. One of the first public "fairies' balls" was held in 1869 at Lodge 110, the Rockland Palace Ballroom, on the corner of 155th Street and Eighth Avenue. Soon similar balls started happening throughout Harlem, and then in cities across the country.

In the 1920s and '30s, stories about the drag balls in Harlem started cropping up in the news, with headlines like "Fag Balls Exposed," "Pansies Cavort," and "Lads Turn Lassies." The tone was shock mixed with utter delight, a shift from the total condemnation of the past century. At the height of 1920s and '30s ball culture, up to eight thousand guests were attending a single event, drawn to the dancing, drag, mirrored balls, drinking, and famed costume competitions.

As expressions of queerness became more mainstream, language began to shift accordingly. The pioneer of many early changes in Europe was a researcher named Magnus Hirschfeld, who established the Institut für Sexualwissenschaft (Institute for Sexual Research) during the Weimar Republic in Germany. My mom was actually the one who introduced me to Hirschfeld and his groundbreaking movie *Anders als die Andern* (*Different from the Others*) when she took a course in "LGBTQ cinema" at the Urbana, Illinois, senior center while I was in college.

"Tante Magnesia," or "Auntie," is what the young queers called Hirschfeld. He said the inspiration for his work was the fact that there were so many like-minded queer people from around the world who simply lacked shared terminology. Hirschfeld met with Indigenous trans people (including spiritual healers) imprisoned at the human zoo inside the Große Berliner Gewerbeausstellung (the Great Industrial Exposition of Berlin). He later visited Black drag balls on a trip to Chicago for further research. Tante Magnesia was the first to attempt to weave together accounts of queer existence all over the world in a positive light. His research proved that queerness occurred naturally around the world, and it shook the framework of European cultural imperialism to its core—even though it was that same framework that made his research possible.

We lost all of Hirschfeld's work when the institute was looted and the contents of its library were burned by the Nazis in 1933. They saw Hirschfeld as a threat not only

news of the Harlem Balls

QUEER SEX BUSY PLANNING DRAGS

NEW YORK—The queer sex has deserted the wide-open spaces to remain indoors, busily engaged in designing and making new gowns for the perverted social affairs they hold every year during the month of April.

Three hundred, of both races, regaled in the height of feminine fashions, strolled the length of the Renaissance Ballroom last week vieing for cash prizes.

Our members of the third sex are showing a keenness for blond wigs.

Two more public "drags" are scheduled for the month of April. An Arabian Nights' Ball will be held at the Savoy Ballroom next Saturday. The season will close the following week-end at the Rockland Palace. Babe Baker will officiate.

THE AFRO-AMERICAN, WEEK OF APRIL 23. 1932

"Auntie" Magnesia ♥

because his research rejected their theories of "degeneracy" but also because he himself was Jewish and lived an openly queer life. He escaped to France but died of a heart attack in 1935, before he was able to restore his archives.

After World War II, professional drag entertainers only became more and more popular in Europe and America, with plenty of straight audiences turning up to see the shows, too. There were campy dinner clubs, like my grandma's beloved Finocchio's; Mona's (also in San Francisco), which featured male impersonators; the Jewel Box Club in Miami, original home of the *Jewel Box Revue*, which toured for more than a decade; the My-O-My in New Orleans; Madame Arthur and Le Carrousel in Paris; and many more. Every city had its own traditions! Most of the public, including my grandparents, didn't know (and probably didn't care) if the performers were queer (although they certainly were). For them, drag was a symbol of liberation from old-fashioned (or even fascist) norms, and played into new fashions and fantasies of the time. Freedom was something worth fighting for, and drag represented that in both superficial and profound ways.

Some of these professional performers, even gay or trans ones, refused to call what they did "drag," at least officially. They would use theatrical terms like *travesty*, *mime*, *mimic*, *illusionist*, or *impersonator* to describe their performances onstage. Perhaps these were deflections to distinguish what they did from any potentially illegal queer concepts, and the possibility of queerness in real life. After all, even as drag went mainstream in the twentieth century, life for queer and trans people did not always get easier. Old laws prohibiting "masquerade" or "sodomy" became newly enforced by conservative reactionaries as a way to police queer life as it spilled from the stage to the street.

MR. LYNN CARTER   MISS STORME DELARVARIE

RKO PROCTOR'S THEATRE
(PENTHOUSE)
DOWNTOWN NEWARK
Unlimited Engagement Starts MARCH 1st

THE WORLD'S FOREMOST
FEMALE IMPERSONATORS
YOU WON'T BELIEVE YOUR EYES
AS YOU WATCH THE MOST AMAZING,
MOST GLAMOROUS, MOST EXCITING
DECEPTION IN THE WORLD!!!

The
MOST
UNUSUAL
REVUE
EVER
SEEN

25 MEN
AND
1 GIRL

JEWEL BOX REVUE

EXCITING MUSIC
GLAMOROUS
GORGEOUS COSTUMES
BRILLIANT PRODUCTION

SHOWTIMES:
CONTINUOUS PERFORMANCES

Mona's ashtray

WHERE GIRLS WILL
MONA'S
440 BROADWAY
SAN FRANCISCO
BE BOYS!

The "Jewel Box Revue" 1960s

Barbette, 1920s

Being openly queer put Texan drag aerialist Barbette in professional danger, but it was also part of her brilliance. In 1923, she flew into the air like an "angel, a flower, a bird" (as Jean Cocteau put it), draped in white ostrich feathers with a platinum finger wave, and sent Europe abuzz. Barbette was hailed as a brilliant modern artist by luminaries like Man Ray and Igor Stravinsky. But even acclaim could not protect her. After a show at the London Palladium, Barbette was found by the police in bed with another man and was permanently barred from receiving a work permit in England. She returned to the US by the 1930s, appeared on Broadway in revues, and made guest appearances in many major circuses before later shifting to work as an aerial choreographer and even a drag coach for the 1959 film *Some Like It Hot*. By 1973, Barbette had stopped performing and retired to her sister Mary's house in Texas. She died from suicide by overdose that year and was cremated and buried just a few miles from where she was born, in Round Rock, Texas. The headstone bears just one name: Barbette. I always wonder what Barbette thought about the shifting politics of her era, having seen fortunes change for queer people so many times. If she watched 1970s drag queens like Divine on her TV . . . what on earth did she think of them? (I hope she lived for it.)

By the 1970s, drag was fully in style worldwide. Danny La Rue was one of the world's most famous female impersonators—or "comic in a frock" as she liked to put it—scoring a feature in *Vogue* and spending several decades in the West End and on TV. But attitudes toward queer and trans people on the streets were still abysmal.

In 1972, Britain's chapter of the Gay Liberation Front, a political organization first started in New York after the Stonewall uprising, released a zine that asked: "Why is Danny La Rue a West End institution, when we get kicked out of our flats for wearing a skirt? Apparently it's all right if you're doing it for money, but perverted if you do it for personal satisfaction." There was even discrimination within early gay activism. The Mattachine Society, an early gay rights organization in the United States, began to distance themselves from drag fundraising events as early as the 1950s, and banned all trans expression from their protests, insisting that "gay" and "trans" should be two separate battles. Creating safe spaces for queer and trans people to be themselves without the purpose of entertaining became more vital than ever.

Danny LaRue, 1970s

During this time, while professional performers preferred terms like *impersonator*, nonbinary and trans radicals on the streets were the ones most proudly calling themselves *drag queens*. These were the people being criminalized most by the law. They weren't onstage in huge wigs and gowns and jewels as we might imagine now, but walking around with shaggy hair, bell bottoms, mascara, and just a little powder, serving drag on the streets!

Gay Liberation Front, 1971

Professional performers looked down on the word *drag* for decades. In *Mother Camp*, Esther Newton's groundbreaking study of queens in the 1960s, an anonymous performer she described as a "stage impersonator" explained that a "'drag queen' is sort of like a street fairy puttin' a dress on . . . tryin' to impress somebody, but 'female impersonator' sounds more professional." They went on to explain that "I never wear makeup out on the street because I don't think anyone needs a neon sign telling what they are!"

Perhaps that's the same reason why Sylvia Rivera, the beloved activist who interrupted the 1973 New York pride parade with calls for trans inclusion, liked

the term *drag queen* so much. "The community is always embarrassed by the drag queens," she later recounted, "but you've got to be who you are. I refuse to pass [for straight]. I couldn't have passed, not in this lifetime."

Raids at gay bars and hangouts had become weekly occurrences, and anyone seen in drag in public was beaten up and carted to jail. Yet these young drag queens, often working-class queer people and queer people of color—changed the future of LGBTQ rights worldwide. Sometimes as young as fourteen, they demanded to be seen as equal and led protests to defend their rights.

Sylvia Rivera, 1996

Later in life, Sylvia Rivera described the night of the Stonewall uprising to Leslie Feinberg in a 1998 interview, explaining, "I didn't really come out as a drag queen until the late '60s. It was street gay people from the village out front . . . then drag queens behind them, and everybody behind us . . . I remember when someone threw a Molotov cocktail, I thought, 'My god, the revolution is here. The revolution is finally here!'"

It was reading these words that made me want to do drag myself, words that showed me why I, too, must dress up and call myself a queen. It wasn't for its theatricality and art, but for its revolutionary spirit that drag appealed to me so strongly. I loved that even when society didn't have room for drag, our queer ancestors made it for themselves.

In Cape Town, South Africa, under apartheid law, Kewpie—a drag queen also known as "Capucine"—made one such space. During the day she ran a hair salon in the all-Black neighborhood of Kensington, and at night, her salon became a center of life for queer people of color. Using the mirrors to

Kewpie, 1967

put on their makeup and style their hair in fantasy updos, they would get ready for the popular drag shows (or "moffie" concerts). They lived, put on shows, shared resources, and survived.

Similarly, in Harlem in the 1970s, Crystal LaBeija revived the ball scene (which had been dormant since World War II) and created a lasting platform for queer Black and Brown stars to be seen and appreciated. The new ballroom scene continued to refine terminology around drag, coining new categories to describe themselves that we still love: *realness*, *voguing*, *face*, and so on.

Some think these histories of revolution have no connection with today's fabulous lips and lashes, rose petals and stilettos. But the struggle is inextricable from the art. Dressing in drag will always be political because it can never be separated from the history and lives of the people who make it. We want our stories to be seen as universal as everyone else's. Through drag, we find clever ways to change the narrative and make room for ourselves.

Kewpie, 1979

M.Y. CRYSTAL LA BEIJA
Crystal La Beija

Everyone is in some kind of drag. Wasn't it RuPaul who said, "You are born naked and the rest is drag"? Or as the Bard, William Shakespeare (or one of his ghostwriters), famously wrote, "All the world's a stage and everyone upon it is just a cross-dresser," or something like that? Drag holds up a mirror to the performativity of every single person. I don't think any of us is ever "just being ourselves"—we are constantly putting on an idea of who we are, posturing and pretending for others and even ourselves to the point that it almost seems useless to pin down what's "real."

But for many of us who do drag, what we wear isn't a metaphor. Drag gives us the opportunity to create crucial realities beyond gender, ones that may not be able to be fulfilled offstage. For some, drag is about expressing our true selves. For others, it's about embodying heritage and ancestry or our own ideas of beauty and ugliness. For others still, it's just about being shocking, raising our voices, or having fun. No matter the inspiration or theme, in drag you cannot separate the art from the artist—it takes place on the stage of our bodies. Drag is a demonstration of the infinite flexibility of our imaginations, and a declaration that what we do with our bodies is ours to decide.

When I was growing up in the 1990s, drag as a metaphor was on sale everywhere. Madonna was popularizing voguing around the world as a symbol of modern life, and Calvin Klein and *Paper* magazine were using imagery of the Club Kids—New York's post-Warhol, gender-bending, nightlife set—to sell city-themed T-shirts to the suburbs . . . even as some of the very people who created the artwork were sick or dying from AIDS. Although queerness was becoming legally decriminalized in America, many straight people were fearful of being around anyone who even looked gay.

But they still wanted to consume our culture. In TV shows and films, queer stories were stolen and portrayed by actors; our signature makeup got mopped by beauty brands to sell products; our catchphrases entered common slang and advertising; our gender-pushing fashions sashayed their ways onto the runway and into the marketplace. Yet only a few queer individuals from the 1990s and early 2000s ever attained "fame" or even cult status among mainstream viewers. Queer imagery became more famous than any queer person.

RuPaul is one of the few icons who got a mainstream spotlight during the 1990s, perhaps because she specifically set out to tap into the obsession with queer culture and work it for her own advantage. She cited Madonna and Princess Diana as her mentors in the art of media manipulation. Purposefully weaving together several different strains of drag—"Female impersonator" mixed with Club Kid, a dash of 1990s ball culture, and a pageant wig—RuPaul shaped herself into her own version of superstar.

I first saw RuPaul on an episode of *Sister, Sister* with Tia and Tamera

Mowry. I still hadn't learned the word "drag," and I thought Ru was just a beautiful giant woman. Yet a part of me still knew there was something special about her, this "Amazonian" woman with unstoppable charm.

Drag reflects society's most pervasive fantasies, and Ru is undoubtedly the embodiment of classic beauty. But for so many of us queer kids, she also broke the mold by forging success and visibility in a way that hadn't been seen in our lifetimes—someone beyond gender, and still thriving! Without RuPaul, drag would not look like this today. It is because of her achievements that I myself have had some huge opportunities . . . even the possibility of writing this book.

RuPaul's Drag Race first appeared in 2009 (and it's still going strong). As the story goes, RuPaul's longtime collaborators Tom Campbell, Fenton Bailey, and Randy Barbato pitched her the idea of making a drag parody of reality TV competitions like *America's Next Top Model*. Ru's only concern: to make sure the show was campy and funny but not mean-spirited or mocking. It worked! Today, *Drag Race* has become the most successful mainstream media crossover from queer culture . . . probably of all time. It has given opportunities to hundreds of drag artists from all across the world to show off their talents and share their voices. With franchises in more than ten countries, *Drag Race* has positioned itself as the go-to source for drag queens in pop culture. Queen by queen, Ru literally built herself a drag empire (funny, we keep coming back to imperialism)!

I watched the first season of *Drag Race* in rapture while I was living in Moscow on a Fulbright research scholarship. I was twenty-one and loved reality shows. I downloaded the episodes through illegal torrents and gagged over BeBe Zahara Benet, Ongina, Nina Flowers, and, later, Raven and Raja. I recommended *Drag Race* to everyone I met; I wanted to see it take over!

Although I had never stopped dressing in drag for myself, I didn't fully understand how vastly drag could change my life, and how this art in particular could reach so many people. *Drag Race* has continued to shift my life and unravel preconceptions.

Seven years later I got a call from executive producer Mandy Salangsang that I had been accepted into the cast of Season 9 . . . My hands were trembling with excitement and I was speechless. "Are you serious?" I asked and later whispered an emotional "thank you" before hanging up the phone to begin planning my costumes. I practiced my runway walk in the same bathroom where my partner, Johnny, and I had filmed my audition tape on a cell phone—back and forth between the window and the wall under the glow of a Home Depot clip lamp. I was determined to make an impression with whatever I had.

I had so much I wanted to share with the world, and planned to use every opportunity to my full advantage. I tried to channel any voices rooting for my downfall (including those in my own head) into a passion and intensity that couldn't be stopped. *You just can't keep a good queen down*, I told myself, and staring into that chipped and paint-stained bathroom mirror, I vowed to keep coming back, no matter what.

In 2017, at the start of the most conservative presidency in recent American history, the ninth season of *RuPaul's Drag Race* broke all previous records for viewership by transferring to VH1. It was an undeniable hit. Audiences at drag shows increased enormously, with unprecedented numbers in attendance. RuPaul's DragCon, a convention dedicated to the show and the queens, sold more than twenty thousand tickets in 2019 alone. And there I was, right in the middle of it, terrified and loving it.

Since then, of course, there have been countless spin-off shows, competing drag competitions, lots of merchandise for sale, and more drag performers than ever. Perhaps aided by the fandom surrounding *RuPaul's Drag Race*, but also through the ease of sharing our art on social media platforms, drag has reached a cultural visibility unlike any other time in history. Drag is the moment!

Unfortunately, while there may be more mainstream interest in drag and more queer representation in the media than ever, many of the people behind the art forms and the real communities we live in are still locked in the fight for equal human rights. Gender expression and sexual identity are not legally protected against discrimination, even here in the US, and many queer and trans people worldwide, particularly trans women of color, experience disproportionate violence and poverty.

Drag, while popular, still doesn't have the same knowledge and research around it as any other art. I once went to an academic lecture about drag where the speakers' only primary sources were episodes of *RuPaul's Drag Race*. No offense, but we can't base our entire understanding of drag around one TV show! While inspiring, the very premise of a reality TV competition is still that we drag queens are infinitely replaceable and disposable.

While *Drag Race* has done so much for queer visibility, I think that local drag scenes abound with queer interventions that deserve our attention, too. *Bushwig* in Brooklyn showcases all genders and styles of drag performance in its yearly festival; *Dragula*, created by the Boulet Brothers in Los Angeles, is a horror drag competition; Switch n' Play in New York places focus on queer women, nonbinary, and trans performers; and more. Local shows often partner with community organizations to raise money for queer and trans people in need, and to support legal battles for equality.

Time and time again it is the local scenes that have uplifted our culture and expanded global knowledge of queer history beyond the Western canon. The drag artists of Beirut, Lebanon introduced me to local icons like Bassem Feghali, who appeared in drag on TV with musical impersonations and comedy for decades. South African queen Belinda Qaqamba Ka-Fassie introduced many to Xhosa drag for the first time. I admire any show or performer who tries to push up against the boundaries of what the "mainstreams" are willing to show, and force us all to reevaluate what our culture includes. That, to me, is the mission of drag!

As alternative styles of drag have grown more popular in local scenes, of course, network shows have tried to adapt and repackage those ideas for mass audiences. No one wants to seem behind the times. But in many ways, the best, most innovative drag will always be a little obscure, outside of the center, just on the verge of being in fashion.

Don't get me wrong: auditioning for *Drag Race* was still the best decision of my life. I do not take for granted the opportunity they gave me to show myself and my work to such a large audience. And I'll never forget what they taught me: how to market and edit my drag in a self-aware way to make it "pop," how to win people over with "smoke and mirrors," and just how many hardworking people it takes behind the scenes to run an empire!

As a result, I have brought my drag around the world, even selling out shows at the Folies Bergères in Paris, the Palladium in London, and the Palace of Fine Arts in San Francisco. I always believed in some small way that my art was good enough, that it deserved to exist and be seen. All I needed was the audience, some lights, and a little magic . . .

In the years I've spent researching the swinging pendulum of drag's sometimes popularity and sometimes marginalization, I've come to believe that drag will always exist, and that it will always push against binaries. I think some people are simply called to put on drag—to inhabit the world between genders, the worlds between the past, present, and future. Others just want a chance in the spotlight, to show as fully as possible who we are and how we can be. Whatever the reason: give us a stage and a little love, and we'll put on one hell of a show for you! (No seriously . . . just give me a stage!)

DRAMA

Anyone can do a reveal. Although it may seem like you need official dispensation to stage a drama, all it really takes is theatricality and a plan. Every single one of us is capable of experimentation, storytelling, and surprise! Perhaps it's a literal reveal—you take off your wig, shock them with a hidden outfit, pull out a prop, get naked. But there are also reveals of a more metaphysical nature—the uncovering of a hidden emotion, a talent, a new perspective. Maybe you reveal something that's been eating away at you—something you just can't hide, something that's hurting, something honest, scandalous, and undeniably true.

If you want to do a "rose petal reveal" and send flowers exploding out of your hands and hair as I did on the finale of *RuPaul's Drag Race*, it is actually quite simple. You just stuff the petals in there and dramatically shake them out! As with all things, it's the details and the execution that really matter.

First, the wig needs to be hairsprayed stiff, with the cleanly trimmed lace glued or taped down snug along the hairline. Thankfully, on the night of the finale we had an expert set of hands in the building: the wigmaker herself, Gloria Divina of Wigs & Grace. Stationed in the dressing room, this drag queen entrepreneur ended up touching up a good twenty wigs or more for all of us in the season cast, packed shoulder pad to shoulder pad in the chorus dressing rooms. She preset my big red wig for me upside down on the table. I filled the cap with petals like it was a bowl before diving in headfirst.

The timing had to be precise. When I'd practiced in my hotel room the night before, I discovered I had to pull the gloves off fast, so the petals traveled in an arc, and I had to shake the wig slowly while lifting it. I knew my heart would be racing, but if you're going to be trembling onstage anyway, you might as well put it to theatrical use!

xoxo ♡ ♡

Backstage, my assistant Cas—a drag king known as Vigor Mortis—held up a Ziploc bag of petals and lifted the back of my wavy wig to stuff more under the mesh cap. "You're too tall!" he said, panicked. "I can't reach!" Then he began sliding fistfuls of the bundled-up petals into my gloves.

"Is that enough?" he asked.

"Oh my god go faster, just stuff more in!" I whispered anxiously.

By that point, we had more than enough. The petals were lumpy inside the gloves and a few were sticking out from beneath the lace of my wig. He picked out the ones along the edge while I took deep breaths.

The audience was cheering. Shea Couleé and I stood backstage, peeking at the stage through a bank of video monitors stacked against the back wall that displayed every camera angle. Peppermint was announced as the winner of the first round of the show's new "Lip Sync for the Crown." I was shocked but delighted. She's a New York City icon, who has grown to be a close friend and the person from *Drag Race* I look up to most. But in that moment, I was in a daze. If she or the fierce, nearly naked (and likely pissed off) Trinity the Tuck walked past, I don't even remember.

"So Emotional," 2017

Shea and I reached out and clasped each other's hands. We would lip-sync against each other in the next round for a shot at the finale. "I'm so proud of us . . . but this fucking sucks." I can't remember who said what. We laughed. We cried. I can't lie . . . it really wasn't pleasant. There we stood, two newfound friends, adults dressed up like pretty dolls, preparing to perform for a shot at $100,000 ($65K after taxes). We wanted to see each other succeed, but that meant the other was immediately going to lose the chance at a big opportunity.

It felt like the stage was growing brighter, pulling us toward its blinding opening. PAs started pushing us forward over sandbags and wires. From the front, the stage looked like RuPaul's open mouth, teeth bared in a snarl as contestants spewed forth. Shea and I strolled out confidently, hand in hand. We knew we had to start serving from the second we hit the stage deck. We were experts at TV now. My eyes felt like they were on fire, burning past my lashes and my fingertips into the ether with an energy that screamed "I AM REAL. I AM HERE." I felt it from Shea, too, vibrating in her fingertips. We were unstoppable.

The music began, Whitney Houston's "So Emotional." Even though I had practiced it over and over, this performance still felt like the first time I'd ever mouthed those fateful words: "*I don't know why I like it . . . I just do.*" I accidentally ripped the entire rose apart on the first downbeat, but it didn't matter. I was tingling with emotions. "*I wish I didn't like it so much . . .*" I looked RuPaul right in her stoic eyes. All I could see was light.

I dedicated the first glove to the TV show itself and threw it ferociously at the cameras, setting off an explosion of petals. I wasn't thinking about winning; I just wanted the chance to perform my heart out.

"*Ain't it shocking what love can do?*" Petals flew into the air as I ripped the second glove off, then spun like a cat to the floor. I started to crawl toward RuPaul, picking up petals with my long, white-marbled nails and flicking them into the crowd. I growled as I stood up and sent my wig flying backward. Rose petals tumbled across my eyes and down my face. I even gnashed my teeth. I stepped forward like a supermodel, transforming into something different, something irrepressible. The final reveal was the biggest I could muster: bald, bold, high-femme ME!

Always so Dramatic

★★★

I was bitten by vampires as a child. Or at least that's what I, living my everyday as a theater piece, told the kids at school. All dramatic children have their origin stories and mine just happened to begin with the undead. The first theater show I ever saw was a marionette adaptation of *Dracula* on a slanted loading dock behind a public library in New Haven, Connecticut. It ended with the puppets pulling the windows wide-open to reveal the sun, trapping Dracula in daylight and burning him to a smoking pile of ash. The drama!

All I knew about vampires at that time came from a few boys at school who loved teasing me for looking like one. As a six-year-old, I was small and pale, with bright blue eyes, dark hair, and occasional melodramatic outbursts. For some reason this read to them as . . . Dracula. (Maybe they hadn't learned any real homophobic slurs yet.)

"Hey, Dracula!"

"I'm going to get my stake!"

"Isn't the sun burning you?"

I probably should have been offended, but I didn't get it. I just answered them truthfully: "I wear lots of sunscreen."

Sitting in the audience of marionette *Dracula*, I learned that I had family connections to the titular Romanian count through my dad's father—Papa Norman. His mother had also emigrated from Transylvania at the turn of the twentieth century. Norman was born during the Great Depression, and his father worked as a scrap hauler and booze runner in downtown Los Angeles. I asked Papa Norman about the Transylvanian side of the family once. "They weren't very nice people," he told me. "The only thing they really cared about was gambling and drinking." They didn't care about living forever. In fact, it seemed that they might have been trying to go quickly.

At age five, I underwent my first vampire transformation for Halloween. My mother helped me paint my face white, and I slicked back my hair with black pantyhose and painted on a wiggly widow's peak. I wore a black turtleneck with a cape, and topped it all off with red eye shadow and yellow vampire teeth.

My mom was so relieved that I finally wanted to dress as a boy that she sewed me a custom sateen vampire cape in black and purple. She was an amazing seamstress, and the cape was exactly what I needed. Long after that Halloween had passed, I would wrap the starched collar around my breast like a bustier, and secretly wear it as a backless evening gown in my room.

For Chanukah that year, my parents bought me a junior adaptation of the book *Dracula*. For a long time, I thought I was reading the real thing—that Gothic novelist Bram Stoker had written a sensible thirty-five-page paperback with big readable type and illustrations. I would later learn that not only was his actual work a rambling beast of a novel, but that he'd practically ripped the concept off from an earlier work by Sheridan Le Fanu called *Carmilla*, where the vampire is a lesbian! My drag sister Miss Malice memorably went in on Bram Stoker's unoriginality over cocktails in Brooklyn one night. I had never heard the full story about the lesbian camp original before, but it does seem awfully telling that a watered-down heterosexual version is what history remembers best now. I might have liked *Carmilla* better, had I known about it. But in 1990s Connecticut, *Dracula* was good enough for me, and my love for it slowly caught on. I was soon lending my book out to classmates, and we were playing "vampire" during recess, where we mimed sucking each other's blood and transforming into the undead. It was like a slow, mouth-to-neck game of tag with no running and lots more drama.

If I saw a group of six-year-olds doing this to each other today, I'd be horrified. But at the time, it was everything! Playing vampire was about dressing up and losing ourselves in character, sharing a fantasy with a community of others who wanted to do the same. As it turns out, the impromptu "vampire club" mostly attracted smart nerdy girls. To this day, I still find that my best friends are

I VANT TO SUCK YOUR BLOOD!

women, butches, and femmes with a touch of the vampiric and an intense commitment to the things they love.

Playacting as a vampire was what got me hooked on theater. At age seven, I decided to write and create a production of *Dracula* in my backyard for a group of neighborhood children to perform. I first tried to write my own script, but it turned out too camp—I accidentally wrote too much romantic tension between the male characters. So I adapted a new one from a dramatization in a library book. I typed it up using my dad's green-and-black-screened computer, printed pages out, and distributed it to the cast. I was going to play Professor Van Helsing because the neighbor boy Will, who lived over the backyard fence, wanted to play Dracula, and my mom told me to be generous. (Also I might have had a little crush on him.)

"Dracula" in the backyard, 1994

We turned the backyard swing set into a proscenium theater. My mom sewed a curtain out of two sheets on her sewing machine, and I dyed it black in buckets in the driveway (the end result was a watercolor gray). My dad ran extension cords from the house and plugged metal clip lamps in as footlights. We carried out the brown living room couch, which I asked for as the only set piece.

I recently asked my dad why they did so much to help me. He put it quite simply: "You didn't often know what you wanted," he told me. "So when you did, we felt that we had to give it a try!" That's some seriously good parenting—observant, a healthy amount of indulgence, and just a little shady. They encouraged me to be myself while still practicing a little self-critique, and they rarely made me feel shame for my ambitions. I couldn't have asked for anything more (which they certainly reminded me of later on!).

My dad and I went around our little neighborhood to staple handmade posters for the show on telephone poles and at the library bulletin board. On the night of the performance we charged a dime admission to everyone's parents and a few curious neighbors.

my Parents

It was my first-ever "Jaenicke Lane Production"—named after the street we lived on. The cast was so nervous that we had to hold on to our scripts during the show, and we mostly spoke too quietly . . . but I just chose to see it as room for improvement. Nothing could ruin my big break!

in the tub, 1994

In high school, my teachers took us to see a masked production of Sophocles's *Oedipus Rex*, from the fifth century BCE, at the local university. We were taught that all drama began in ancient Greece, a development from ritual costumed dances to Dionysus (which I only learned as an adult had involved so much drag). To my surprise, *Oedipus* was the most boring and traumatizing experience I'd ever had in a theater. There was no style or conviction, no truly dramatic moments, and we couldn't even see their faces. Just lots of togas and halfhearted chanting about fate and sex. I was livid when Jocasta's death scene—which I'd been looking forward to for the entire show—happened offstage, denying us what could have been the production's one truly sublime moment! The most delightful part was when Oedipus gouged his eyes out, the actor's white mask opening to reveal two red-sequined pools of blood. But it was still disappointing to think that the origin of theater was just a man monologuing to himself about incest.

Of course the Greeks didn't really invent drama; they only claimed they did. In truth, the development of theater happened independently all over the world. It would be more accurate to say that drama, performance, and art began with Indigenous rituals around the world. Shamans and storytellers had vital cultural roles, dramatizing histories and myths so that their audience could understand where they came from and their place in the world. They passed down cultural ideals and knowledge through performance, which regularly involved drag.

Some of the oldest recorded examples of ancient drama can actually be found in India, where sacred folk dances evolved into Sanskrit drama and classical dance, a narrative performance art that was formalized in treatises such as the Natya Shastra, dating back as far as 500 BCE. Likewise across Africa, masked dramas and rituals were widespread, with performers lining up for a chance to lose themselves in the reenactment of mythological characters, animals, or ancestors.

One of my favorite styles of ancient drama is the Barong dance, a folk performance that has been enacted outside temples in Bali for millennia. In the yearly performance, the most evil masked character is always a drag role—a white, hairy, saggy-breasted witch with red eyes named "Rangda." Some thought the Rangda masks were possessed with dangerous magical feminine energy that could harm the performers if not handled correctly (which led them to restrict women from the role).

a dancer dressed as Rangda) ↓

The ancient Greeks did help establish drama as a popular art form rather than a religious event, and in doing so advanced a number of corresponding technical innovations: theater architecture, stagecraft, lighting design, and scripts to document the shows. The Greeks were also among the first to place an outright ban on women in drama, claiming that women's minds weren't strong enough to distinguish fantasy from reality. They created laws that perpetuated the message that women were biologically "inferior," and reinforced this thinking through the plots of their plays, the way the characters spoke, and even the gendered designs of the masks. Misogynistic prejudice has often hindered the development of the arts. Although the restriction of women initially led to more drag roles for the remaining male actors, it ultimately limited the creative potential. By implying that there were essential differences in men's and women's capabilities or minds, the Greek theatrical traditions only reinforced the binary. The

Boo!

same happened with other theaters of empire, including the European mystery plays, performed during church feast days, which featured drag roles primarily as a means to restrict women from taking part.

Although there was never an official law banning women from English stages, by the 1600s, all-male performances were the norm in professional theaters. "Boy players," generally between the ages of ten and twenty, were recruited to play female roles, and the management of these actors grew into a well-established industry. Although many people pinpoint this as the moment when drag originated . . . I don't see it. These young actors were usually orphans or had been kidnapped from poor families to work long hours in big, uncomfortable costumes, with wages handed over to their managers for a huge percentage cut. These were not conditions for personal expression and therefore not true drag.

HELP!

Outside Europe, gender-inclusive theater was still happening, and better resembled the spirit of drag. In Japan, a drag king named Okuni, a temple dancer and sex worker, is believed to have invented Kabuki theater in the early seventeenth century. *Kabuku* meant "off-kilter" or "crooked," and Okuni fully embodied the word's queer potential. She was said to have appeared onstage dressed as a man, with a huge sword by her side, singing bawdily to drag queens. But in 1629 the Japanese government, yet another empire, instituted laws that restricted women from drama. All the lead femme roles came to be played by drag queens called *onnagata*. Although many geishas of the time said that they looked to the *onnagata* for inspiration of heightened femininity, the institutions of drama were closed to them.

Whenever theaters did accept women onstage, drag was free to take on new personal meanings and expressions. In 1914, a few decades after women were finally allowed to appear on Japanese stages again, the Takarazuka Revue Company (a division of the

drawing of Okuni

Hankyu railway) created a lavish musical production starring all women, including many *otokoyaku*, or "boy roles," drag king pop figures who became beloved throughout the country. The show remains popular to this day.

Takarazuka Revue

In China, formal theatrical traditions also started with both women and men onstage, often in drag. Yet during the 1700s and 1800s, during the Qing Dynasty, women were banned from appearing onstage. In classical Chinese opera, *nandan* performers—men in femme drag—became the stars.

One of the most famous *dans* in modern history is Mei Lan-Fang, who debuted onstage in 1904 at the age of eleven. Mei sang in a high-pitched voice, posed with immaculate expressions, and was known for her "stunts"—including acting drunk and bending backward to the ground with a glass of wine in her teeth. Mei toured worldwide in 1930 and was heralded by luminaries like Sergei Eisenstein and Bertolt Brecht for her technical precision, theatricality, and fantasy costumes. Although offstage Mei presented outwardly masculine, and was married with a wife and children, she was rumored to maintain subtle queer style. She had long hair and nails, and there were many stories about her affairs with powerful warlords of the time. In the late 1930s Mei, a long advocate for the return of women to theater, trained the first women back on Chinese stages and the first Chinese cinema stars. I was given a turquoise Manchu-style dressing gown that was said to belong to her. It remains a prize possession—my favorite part is that I can see sweat stains in the lining. (Even her majesty perspires!)

Mei Lan Fan

During conservative periods throughout history and across cultures, many have echoed the moral condemnations of philosopher Isidore of Seville, who wrote in the early 600s that theatrical drag performers, or *histriones*, "mimicked the goings-on of shameless women." In 1632, William Prynne

Dressing Gown

wrote about boy players in English theater: "This putting on of women's array . . . not only excites many adulterous filthy lusts . . . but likewise instigates them to self-pollution . . . and to that unnatural sodomitical sin of uncleanness." Just like today, these conservative responses were rarely based in truth, often completely making things up to incite public rage. Gay icon and playwright Oscar Wilde tried very hard to find evidence of queer encounters between actors and the theater's wealthy benefactors in Shakespearean times, as many believed there were, but his research yielded nothing conclusive.

Because of the moralistic tone found in many historical records, it can ultimately be hard to distinguish free expressions of queerness from instances of nonconsensual abuse. Violence and coercion underpinned the lives of too many performers, so even though the theater could have been an outlet for queer expression, the life surrounding it was still unjust. Around the world, it was young people caught in the middle who always seemed to face the worst condemnations for the system that was taking advantage of them. In Turkey, young boys enslaved by the Ottoman Empire were trained to perform as *kocek*—drag dancers who were also forced into sex work. Young girls were similarly forced to be *cengi*, belly dancers and occasional drag kings. In Thailand, *kathoey* (or crudely, "ladyboy") was been used to describe a variety of queer people—but although the existence of this "third option" ostensibly allowed a greater cultural tolerance for nonconforming people, pervasive stigma has still given many no other option but survival via sex work or jobs as underpaid nightclub entertainers.

The feared connections between drag and sex might actually tap into some historic traditions, but this is a tradition of the theater as a whole. As drama became a well-developed art across cultures, it also became a business and frequently sold sex. In many ancient societies, the stars of the stage were available for intercourse with wealthy benefactors who invested. Even predating these traditions, Indigenous guides and healers sometimes incorporated sexuality as part of their rituals. For our ancestors, sex with a revered spiritual guide might not have been seen as erotic, but rather a form of worship.

Consensually worship me

But as long as sex remained connected to entertainment, theaters in patriarchal societies had a catch-22 on their hands. If they allowed women onstage, they contradicted paternalistic morals that tried to keep women away from sex work. And when they restricted women from theater, the queer and gay undertones grew more visible.

In 1642, the Puritans won out and shut down all official theaters in London over their fears around boy players. When they reopened eighteen years later in 1660, all female roles were now to be played by women. A legend goes that when the first woman played Desdemona in *Othello* after the ban was lifted, the prologue that night proclaimed: "The woman plays today; mistake me not; no man in gown, or page in petticoat . . . in this reforming age we have intent to civilize our stage." (Meanwhile the role of Othello was being portrayed in blackface— they still had work to do.) European audiences were now encouraged to view drag, and therefore queer expression, as something "uncivilized" and "heathen," part of some ancient sexual history that they consciously needed to suppress. Perhaps drag is a little "uncivilized," its roots tracing back to the earliest human expressions . . . To me, that's what makes it so timeless!

I didn't know about the history of "boy players" when my parents took me to see Shakespeare's *A Midsummer Night's Dream* at a local high school but I became obsessed anyway. I immediately checked out books, rented movie adaptations, and started planning my next neighborhood spectacle.

This time I played the dual roles of Oberon the fairy king and Flute, the cross-dressing "rude mechanical" who gets into drag to portray Thisbe in a play within the play at the end. It was one of the first drag characters I had ever come across and I felt it was written for me. I wore a green cowl and a teal sweatshirt as Flute (originally made by my mom as an iguana costume for Halloween), then as Thisbe, I put on a tangled blond wig and filled my sweatshirt with two big balloon boobs.

We embraced minimalism with the staging, using the swing set again, but this time with a rope ladder hanging down and no curtain—just the blooming yellow forsythia bush behind us. Green lights from the clip lamps cast an eerie glow over the entire set and on the night of the show, it misted.

I made sure the dramatic peak of our production came during my death scene as Thisbe. When she stabs herself, I passionately punctured each of my giant balloon boobs with a cardboard dagger (and a hidden safety pin).

"Adieu!" (*Pop.*)

"Adieu . . ." (*Poke poke POP.*)

"Adieu!" I collapsed dead on the ground. With that, the audience gave me my first standing ovation.

★★★★

Cities saved the arts, especially drag. Modernization in the eighteenth and nineteenth centuries, with advances in transportation and later electricity, helped cities like New York, Tokyo, London, and Paris become hubs of diverse life. Cultural exchange prompted new developments in thought, and queer life began to flourish alongside it, as people from all classes and backgrounds congregated together. Different theater traditions began to interact with each other, too, creating blended forms like variety shows, comic opera, and vaudeville.

"Thisbe"

"Midsummer Night's Dream," 1995

One of the biggest drag successes of the mid–Victorian era was Charles H. Du Val, who debuted a one-man show called *Odds & Ends* in the 1860s. Born to a family of Irish musicians and entertainers, Du Val developed a routine where he quick-changed between more than twenty different characters, including Mrs. Clearstarch and Betsy Scrubbe (Irish cleaning ladies), Signor Howlini (the tenor), Professor Dullbore (the burlesque lecturer), and Colonel Peppard (stationed in India). Du Val was particularly inventive

DuVal, 1883

Get ready for the... REVEAL...

with the technological secrets behind his reveals, using a quick-rigging system to go between Mephistopheles, Faust, and Marguerite in seconds (and switching octaves while singing), or using oil paintings with the faces cut out to "become" various living portraits. Reviewers all favored one character in particular: Bella Dashaway, a bedazzled debutante in a ball gown of the latest style.

His show toured from Europe to colonial outposts in Africa, India, Ceylon (Sri Lanka), and throughout his home country of Ireland, accompanied by a crew of two: his wife, the socialite Mary Dorcas Burke ("Minnie"), and a personal photographer to document it all. A journalist of the time wrote that "every one has read or heard of the famous entertainer at one time or another . . . Wherever he goes he is welcomed as a bon camarade. [People] look upon him with great respect, as one who has breathed the mystic perfumes of the footlights."

Even though history views Du Val as a cis straight man, I sense some distinctive queer codes at play. After a performance in Pretoria, South Africa, his tour was interrupted by the onset of the First Boer War. Now stranded there, Du Val grew a mustache (since his drag had been put on pause) and started self-publishing a thrice-weekly newspaper for the British troops called *News of the Camp: A Journal of Fancies, Notifications, Gossip and General Chit Chat*. The zines, which mixed news, cartoons, and examples of "camp life" (in all the senses of the word), were truly ahead of their time in capturing a distinctively queer self-aware snark and humor in the face of crisis.

Unfortunately Du Val's life was cut short. He died in February 1889, at the age of forty-two. He was headed on his biggest world tour yet, with planned visits to the Americas for the first time, when he fell off a ship and drowned. His wife claimed it was an accident . . . others said it was suicide.

By the turn of the twentieth century, variety shows developed into the first "follies," and those in turn shaped the modern musical. It was in this exciting era of popular theater that a young Josephine Baker got her start as a chorus dancer. Living in Harlem during the 1920s, Josephine was exposed to a thriving queer scene, including the famous Rockland Palace drag balls and stars of the era like Gladys Bentley. In 1925, she joined a Parisian troupe where her own brand of African fantasy burlesque became an overnight sensation.

Josephine Baker

While her feminine iconography is its own kind of drag, she was also celebrated for a classic male impersonation act. It's no surprise that she adored drag queens, and was known to be a frequent guest of Finocchio's and the *Jewel Box Revue*. Baker also used her international platform as a tool for activism, working as a spy for France to take down the Nazis, and later speaking out against racism in the US at the 1963 March on Washington.

Baker watched the tides of fashion and politics turn several times in her lifetime. The conservatism of the 1930s had sent drag underground—the Hays Code restricted any overtly queer content or cross-dressing in popular film. That's why the only place to see drag for decades were clubs and dinner theaters that had mafia connections (including Finocchio's and the Stonewall), or in touring performances by international artists like Mei Lan-Fang or Barbette.

But by the more radical 1960s and '70s, drag was back on stage and screen: Warhol, Divine, Danny LaRue and more. In Tokyo, drag comedian Akihiro Miwa became famous for a bawdy song called "Me Que Me Que," then started appearing in films and hosted and starred in a monthly drag show in the Shibuya district. The show, called *Akihiro Miwa no Sekai* (*The World of Akihiro Miwa*), was full of ballads, comedy songs, and guest stars, and ran into the 2000s.

In Mexico City, a queen named Francis got her own show in the height of the 1970s—*Francis: La Fantasía*

Akihiro Miwa, 1960

Hecha Mujer (*The Fantasy Made Woman*), at the famous Teatro Blanquita, and it ran for seventeen years to great acclaim.

But even the most famous drag acts throughout history have still often been seen as a novelty, a "side" show. Perhaps today, as openly queer people step into positions of power throughout the world, things could change for good. Audiences and investors alike could adjust their views and tastes, and bring queer stars into the spotlight where we belong!

Off the main stages, in gay bars and cafes, however, is where some of drag's biggest innovations have taken place and likely will continue. Jukeboxes started becoming popular in the 1950s, which made the first lip-sync performances possible. Although there's no single known origin of the drag lip-sync, I can certainly imagine how it began: an impromptu performance from a queen who knew the words to a song on the jukebox and wanted to seize the moment. By the 1960s, the craze of "record shows"—full-production lip-syncs—had caught on. In the 1972 book *Mother Camp*, Esther Newton noted that initial reactions to lip-syncing were quite divided. To the generation still obsessed with classical "impressionists," record shows seemed like cheap tricks.

But nonetheless, New York's Club 82, London's Madame Jojo's, and Paris's La Grande Eugène became renowned internationally for clever lip-sync performances. And the influx of new performers brought new styles of drag that was outside of typical beauty standards—punk, overtly queer, and even politically radical.

With less focus on the production of music thanks to developments in creative-arts technologies, other aspects of the shows could shine for the first time. By the

Francis

enjoying the spotlight

but will it last?

The Unique
CLUB 82
82 EAST 4th STREET
NEW YORK CITY
PRESENTS...
Fun - Fair For '57

PRODUCED, STAGED
AND DIRECTED BY
KITT RUSSELL

Club 82
Program, 1957

1970s, artists were incorporating sound effects, video, lighting, and more, always using the newest inventions within performances and adding a creative flair. Experimental theater and nightclubs owe a lot to the gay bar, and to the surreal drag shows that were thrown together on its stages.

Troupes like San Francisco's Cockettes, founded by the drag queen Hibiscus, became famous worldwide for their unrehearsed and chaotic theater pieces. When the Cockettes came to perform in New York in 1971, attendees including Andy Warhol and Angela Lansbury got up and left midway, followed by most of the audience, turned off by the messy style and disorganization. Only one performer continued onstage . . . Sylvester. She made a joke about the mess of a show and kept right on singing. Backed by Martha Wash and Izora Rhodes, with producers and record companies in full tow, Sylvester stayed in New York and made a name for herself as the "Queen of Disco." Yet even still, Sylvester struggled to find lasting success as a queer artist in the 1980s, first facing the racist and homophobic "disco sucks" movement and later dying of AIDS.

The "Cockettes," 1969

Time and again, queer, working-class, and Black nightlife spaces have been where culture and artistry grows, but they aren't often treated with the same respect. Disco, house, and club music all grew out of queer Black nightlife, as did the modern nightclub, sound systems, and many trends in popular fashion. The two legendary DJs who brought disco and house to wider audiences, Larry Levan and Frankie Knuckles met while beading a dress for a Harlem-based drag queen named The Duchess. Levan's parties at Paradise Garage inspired generations of clubs and music traditions. We wouldn't have today's pop culture without our queer legends.

Sylvester, 1972

New York in particular has had more than its fair share of underground, high-concept drag acts. The Theater of the Ridiculous, produced in connection with Warhol's Factory, starred cult figures like Jackie Curtis, Charles Ludlam, and Mario Montez in drag roles. The popularity of those shows helped set the stage for later New York–based troupes like Hot Peaches (with performers like International Chrysis), Les Ballets Trockadero de Monte Carlo (which staged camp ballets en pointe), and many more.

Even experimental film looked to New York drag. American filmmakers like John Waters and Jack Smith developed cult followings for their independent camp masterpieces, which featured drag inspired by the queer scenes around them.

Waters's most iconic star, Divine, was posthumously called "the most important drag queen of the century" by *People* magazine and was celebrated as an ultimate example of postmodern identity. Off her film successes she launched a disco and nightlife career, touring around the world, where she became known for outlandish stunts onstage such as rising up on a hydraulic lift, singing on the roof of a boat, riding a baby elephant, and of course screaming at the audience. She served as an inspiration for many—from the character design for Ursula the Sea Witch in Disney's 1989 film *The Little Mermaid* to the ethos of the punk drag superstars who came after. But in Glenn Milstead's own lifetime, he was unhappy with the way he was treated as "Divine," wishing he could be seen less as a drag queen and more as a serious actor.

Divine, 1981

Ethyl Eichelberger

By the 1980s, the world of theater was starting to take certain creators like Harvey Fierstein, Ethyl Eichelberger, and Charles Busch more seriously—they led their own movements in drag as theater. Many artists of the time picked up and remixed old drag tropes to brilliant new effect: the quick-change artist, the pantomime dame, the diva, and so on, but with new contexts and materials.

Cabaret and club artists like Kevin Aviance, Justin Vivian Bond, and Vaginal Davis went from performing in gay bars to being written

Kevin Aviance

about as the epitome of experimental brilliance and playing the biggest stages in the world (including Carnegie Hall).

My biggest New York drag inspiration is undoubtedly Lypsinka, who harnessed early remixing technology in the 1980s and '90s to create groundbreaking and passionate performances using a collage of vintage music, sound effects, and movie and TV quotes. After she performed in several of fashion designer Thierry Mugler's iconic early runways and videos, her unique lip-sync style became even more popular worldwide and is even imitated to this day by many drag performers.

Lypsinka

Unfortunately, for much of their careers, many of these legends were treated like amateurs by the artistic institutions that looked to them for inspiration and revenue. From the sound of it, they were sometimes paid like amateurs behind the scenes. Being a professional drag artist may sound punk and glamorous, but many find it almost impossible to make a living doing it. Even today, I worry we're all just a few lost gigs away from going broke!

★ ★ ★ ★

My first time on a professional stage was for an alien invasion. It was 1995. I was eight years old and was cast in Len Jenkin's *Pilgrims of the Night* at the Yale School of Drama. The show was an adaptation of Chaucer's *The Canterbury Tales* transposed to a modern-day alien crash site. I had a bit part as a nerdy kid who sees an extraterrestrial goddess one day while walking alone with his stuffed monkey. Then, as an adult (played by another actor), he is visited again by the goddess, this time disguised as a sex worker, and he confesses to her that the childhood sighting changed the course of his life.

PILGRIMS OF THE NIGHT

A PLAY BY LEN JENKIN

DIRECTED BY:
DAVID KARL LEE

YALE SCHOOL OF DRAMA
UNIVERSITY THEATRE · 222 YORK STREET
DECEMBER 15-20

"Pilgrims of the Night," 1995

When I found out about the audition—posted in the hall of school—I had to beg and plead my mom to let me try out. She was the opposite of a stage parent, always discouraging me from taking on too much.

"They are very unlikely to cast you, Sashinka. Do not get your hopes up. You probably don't even have time to do this alongside your schoolwork."

Still, she let me go through with it, and gave me a power grip to encourage me. Her "power grips" were when we would link our hands and dig fingernails into each other's palms. Sometimes it hurt a little because she kept her nails filed into almond shapes, unpainted, sharp. But pain just meant the power was really working!

There were about fifteen boys in the audition, and I was the shortest. I thought I'd nailed my line reading and returned home already practicing the lines. The next night we got a phone call from the director on our landline. "We'd like to offer Sasha the role, but we need to warn you that the play has adult themes." There was sex, swear words, naked breasts, zombie slaves, and "Olga the Headless Woman." I fit right in!

Grandma Dina was so proud of me for getting the part that she flew all the way from California for opening night. She even brought a trophy in the shape of an acrylic star engraved with "Best Actor: Sasha Steinberg" and presented it to me after the show, along with a bouquet of roses and happy tears in her eyes. To this day, I keep her trophy next to my *Drag Race* crown to remind me of her. In many ways, it's even more precious to me because that small moment of recognition was what inspired me to shoot for the stars.

"I only got one job as an actress," Grandma Dina told me that night, "and the other girls always teased me. Some of the other chorus girls even poured sand in my hair at the beach! But they stopped when an actress named Carol stood

up. She said, 'Don't ruin her hair, Dina has to do a show tonight!' Nicest thing anyone ever did for me. You should always be sweet to the people around you. Remember, it's their night, too. Anyway, that girl Carol grew up to be a star . . . Carol Channing! And she would have loved you!"

The year after my stage debut, we moved from Connecticut to Illinois. My parents hadn't intended to be nomadic, but there weren't that many jobs available for a German translator and a professor of the history of the Russian Revolution. I was wrecked by our departure, sad to lose my backyard stage, and I kissed my chances of starring on Broadway goodbye.

When we arrived in Illinois, however, my mom heard about a student play that needed a young actor to play a four-hundred-year-old vampire stuck in a young boy's body. The actor would have to be "staked" and then lie dead, covered in blood, onstage for ten minutes. *Are you kidding?* I felt like it was written for me!

The writers were both at the audition, a queer duo dressed in ferocious mid-1990s gothic wear with twelve-plus piercings each and nearly identical cropped, bleached, and colorfully dyed hair. The music and script were original, though largely based on the Anne Rice universe. They asked me to sing the character's main song in a crisp boy soprano.

"Come play with me, you needn't be afraid . . . I'll take you on a journey far away!"

I felt the fantasy and gave it my all, even though I was shaking with nerves. That night I got the call: I got it!

Their show, *Scarlet Lines*, introduced me to another side of the Midwest beyond the farmers and custard stands and Mennonite desk makers (although I love those, too). They introduced me to farm goths in black fishnets, leather chokers, and fantasy hair. Despite our age difference, they made me feel like

"Scarlet Lines," 1997

SHOWS! TONIGHT

I could fit in with them, and as a result, that I would fit into my new home of Illinois, too. They even told me about the store where I could buy my very own eyeliner, studded dog collar, or silver rings. (My mom took me there, but only let me buy incense and a hemp necklace.)

Passionate community theater like this showed me that it was possible to organize a show without any institutions giving you permission. If you really love an art and want to make innovations, you have to be prepared to set out on your own and build your own stage. It is often the work at the fringes, created by people who have no choice but to innovate and take risks, that bring about the most exciting new ideas. Theater that isn't built for profit will always be more forward-thinking. Amateur theatrics will always have more space for a wide variety of people, and a wide variety of drag. In my experiences since, working outside the mainstream contemporary theater and drag systems has had its advantages, pushing me to find new models for creating shows, new values surrounding priorities and resources, and new strategies for making my ideas pop.

My entire extended family came to see me perform as Sol the four-hundred-year-old vampire—Grandma Dina and Papa Norman flew in and slept on our pullout couch. The queers of the cast connected to my grandma immediately. They all sat in a circle backstage laughing and hugging, exchanging stories. On the car ride home she giggled to herself. "I'm still a fag hag!" she confessed.

One month later, Grandma Dina died in the middle of the night from an unexpected heart attack. It was abrupt, and my first great loss. I stayed up until school the next morning, sobbing. Later that year, when the cast album was self-released, the writers of the show added a special note to the booklet: "Dedicated to Dina Steinberg."

Beautiful relationships don't need to last forever to make deep shifts in your life; they can move inside and live on through reflection and imagination. I still think about Dina often and wonder what she'd think about me. "She'd be the president of the Sasha Velour Fan Club," my aunt tells me without hesitation. I suppose in some ways she was the founding member, with her trophy and rose bouquet, cheering me on.

The finale of Season 9 of *RuPaul's Drag Race* was filmed the night of June 9, 2017, exactly two years from the day I saw my mom for the last time. RuPaul asked me onstage what my mom, the incomparable Jane Hedges, would have thought of seeing me up there. I laughed—I could imagine her and so many other spirits right by my side. I saw both of my grandmas smiling. I tried to imagine Du Val, Mei Lan-Fang, Josephine Baker, and Divine there, too. I'd be nowhere without my inspirations, without the people who give me context..

My costume for the final interview portion was a huge blue lace re-creation of Eiko Ishioka's Bride of Dracula gown from the Francis Ford Coppola film *Bram Stoker's Dracula*. It was created by the brilliant Diego Montoya—a Peruvian-born, Miami-raised Brooklyn artist whose designs inspired me long before we finally started collaborating. It was the biggest, most impractical thing I had ever tried on, and I was in heaven wearing it.

I knocked the stool over when I first tried to sit down and started overheating so much they had to send out drag makeup legend Raven to powder my forehead before I started answering Ru's

"RuPaul's Drag Race," 2017

49

questions. Raven rolled her eyes as I apologized (and sweated) profusely. The collar was strangling me, partly because I had to stick a screwdriver and a ruler up the back to make it stand up the right way, but the discomfort was worth it for the drama.

So there I was, slowly being killed by this gown, sweating under the lights, and fully determined to make it all look effortless. What would my mom say?

"Too MUCH!" I winked.

Ru laughed. (Always try to make Ru laugh.)

In truth, I thought that my mom would be surprised and proud to see that she had raised such a fine lady. I missed her. She was a great listener, a careful speaker, and a truly kind soul. She helped build up my confidence so I could realize my dreams, but she was hard on me, too, teaching me to work for what I wanted, and to be realistic about my limitations. I thought about her power grips and, squeezing my own hands tight, I could almost feel her.

No matter what happened, I felt like a winner from the crowd's response to the first lip-sync. Even if Ru sent me home, I was okay leaving having shared my very best. When she announced I would "shantay" and told Shea to "sashay," I felt disappointment and excitement mixed into one. But before we could say anything to each other, a snap of Ru's finger swept us both through the replica of her open mouth and backstage in different directions.

I think that's when Bob the Drag Queen stepped out from behind the monitors, crown and pillow in hand, dryly remarking, "I called it. You just made history." I was a puddle of emotion, though, running downstairs right into Peppermint. We screamed, perhaps a bit giddy that the finale would be a battle of the underdogs—both well aware that we didn't have the biggest fan support at that point. Production gave us about a minute to change into our final looks of the season. Mine was white neoprene, with see-through white-on-white giraffe print, white paillettes, and ostrich feathers, another Diego Montoya creation.

He had pulled this last costume together overnight. Less than a week before I flew to Los Angeles for the finale, the producers told us that we'd need an extra

performance look if we made it through to the final lip-sync battle. I knew I wanted something all white, like a futuristic alien, with a mask that cracked apart mouth first. Diego came up with the details. He had to make the mask twice the night before the flight because he forgot to account for my gigantic nose. Fully dressed, I couldn't see anything, but I felt like royalty. I gave myself a spritz of my mom's favorite perfume for good luck (Carner Barcelona), zipped up my Pleaser boots, and ran out of the dressing room.

PAs escorted Peppermint and me to the back of the house so we could dramatically enter down each aisle. We were both jogging uphill on the carpet hallway now, dressed in our sequins and ostrich feathers and stones—her in a short pussycat wig, me completely covered in the crystal egg mask—some badass trans dinosaur shit. We could hear the rumble of the audience behind the doors. The final countdown began.

I peeked through the doors at the back of the house to get a glimpse of the stage. I tried to see through cracks in my mask as they swept my wig and rose petals into a tangled pile on the side of the stage. Then they brought some "stand-ins" onto the stage—two guys in cheap blond wigs, smeared with a bit of lipstick. They started playing Whitney's "So Emotional" again—this time at half volume,

Me & Peppermint Backstage

as the stand-ins attempted to reenact our lip-sync while the cameras captured reaction shots of the audience and of Ru. I felt like I shouldn't be watching, but I couldn't stop.

A producer prompted the audience on a loudspeaker: "Now let's react to Sasha's big reveal . . ."

The crowd went wild and stood up again. I could only see the back of her head, but I wondered if Ru was reacting more than she had to the real thing. The next day, while we filmed the reunion, I found one of the guys who did these performances and talked to him by the craft services table.

"Yeah, babe! I did these all season to get reaction shots. Ru loves it when we just make total fools of ourselves!"

For a second it started to depress me that my hero was more excited about amateur scare drag than the carefully planned performance I had spent my entire life preparing for. But that's a showbiz lesson for you: No matter what you are doing, there is always someone doing a ridiculous imitation and getting the reaction you always wanted. This was another fabulous reveal: Your heroes are just people, and TV is all smoke and mirrors. If I were hosting a show, would I want to film fake reactions to get different camera angles? Absolutely! And maybe perfect execution and "trying hard" aren't all they are cracked up to be. Maybe there really is something divine about getting up there and being a complete mess.

costume

Growing up, I believed they lived in the deep recesses of our hallway closet, where my parents kept vintage coats and dresses in dry-cleaning bags. At night, I could hear their cackling from the darkness, the squeaking of wire hangers being pushed to the side, and the creaking of their bones slipping out of a narrow crack in the door. In my nightmares, they hovered along the ceiling, robes fluttering in an invisible wind as they descended toward me, their bony fingers and long nails outstretched toward my neck, surely planning to tickle me to death. I imagined one plucking a plumed feather from Grandma Dina's vintage hat on the top shelf, twisting it toward me tauntingly, wailing mouth growing ever wider, screaming and laughing until I woke up in a sweat. As an adult, I think this sounds fabulous . . . let me dress up as *her*. But at the time, the closeted feminine was terrifying, and it kept coming for me with a vengeance.

Perhaps it's no coincidence that *The Wizard of Oz* was the first movie I ever saw . . . I was four and although I'd peeped a few incomprehensible art films from the hallway after my parents thought I was asleep, this was the first time they sat me in front of the diode TV for some culture. After all, it would be my introduction to Judy Garland: a momentous occasion!

They started to doubt their decision when the Wicked Witch threw her first fireball in Munchkinland and I began screaming at the top of my lungs. My mom gave me a tissue from her purse and I calmed myself down, then asked if we could rewind it and watch it again. On second viewing, my eyes widened and my heart started beating even faster. This time I kept silent and leaned forward toward the TV. I must have been bewitched because apparently all I whispered was "again!"

My love (and fear) of witches escalated quickly from there. I took to dressing up in a black oversize cloak—one of my grandma's castoffs—and flying around the room. I wore my mom's black slip as a wig and hurled imaginary fireballs of my own, whispering in a witch's cackle. "I'll get you, my pretty. And your little dog, too!"

Ha!!

I aspired to the Wicked Witch's Technicolor green skin, her long yellow fingernails, her nose and sharply pointed chin, her corseted silhouette. How could you resist her giant Victorian shoulders, epic hat, and long wavy black hair with its gorgeous tendrils kissing her emerald face? Of course she was a monster, but she was also graceful, stylish, perhaps even beautiful.

All kids are drawn to things that frighten, but witches in particular seem to represent the idea that a certain kind of feminine strength might exist outside our traditional senses of beauty.

The brilliant performer behind the Wicked Witch, Margaret Hamilton, told Fred Rogers in an appearance on *Mister Rogers' Neighborhood* in 1975, that the Wicked Witch "is what we sometimes refer to as 'frustrated'—she's very unhappy because she never gets what she wants. . . . Most of us get something . . . but as far as we know that witch has never got what she wanted. And mainly what she wanted was those ruby slippers, because they're powerful . . ." I already felt a connection with the Wicked Witch's unapologetic strangeness, and I understood even more deeply her frustration that someone had stolen her powerful clothes. I think, ultimately, a witch is neither good nor wicked . . . she just knows what she deserves.

A witch is the ultimate "diva"—a woman with a full range of expression. She feels anger and jealousy, has her own ambitions, and strikes fear into the hearts of those who behold her, threatening to upend the patriarchal social order. Even though myths around witches undoubtedly have misogynistic elements, there is something appealing about them, which speaks to me as a nonbinary person. I, too, feel like someone who explodes and offends the limits of my expected gender.

The next Halloween, I trick-or-treated in our neighborhood as the Wicked Witch. I was allowed a pair of pink jelly sandals to represent my ruby slippers. In my fantasy, the Wicked Witch had gotten the shoes she wanted, and now she didn't have to be so cruel. I didn't realize it at the time, but apparently my

My drawing of a "witch," 1992

costume caused quite a stir on Jaenicke Lane. The little
Catholic girl across the street (also an "Alex," as I was
sometimes called) was dressed as the Wicked Witch,
too, and her parents were horrified that the neighbor's boy
was stealing their darling daughter's thunder. While the adults tensed
up, I took my twin Wicked Witch up the hilly street for a
twirl on our broomsticks. I was happy to be matching her.
My only grudge was that she wouldn't let me try on her red
glitter slippers. She said they were too hard to take off, which
I believed because she clearly couldn't walk in them! And her
parents thought I was the amateur . . .

My beautiful wickedness!

My grandma Dina would always let me play the Wicked
Witch when I dressed up with her. She would play Dorothy, and
would mime lifting and pouring out a heavy bucket of water onto my
head as I shrieked, "I'm melting. Melting! . . . Oh what a world, what
a world!" before crumpling to the ground. Then I'd crawl out of the bottom of
the black dress I was wearing and escape, leaving a tragic puddle of polyester on
the ground. Heartbreaking!

This was my first big reveal act, and I performed it for whoever would watch.
It wasn't a perfect illusion, but I'd like to think that my commitment sold it. My
performance as the Wicked Witch instilled an instant love of clothing—the
power of using a garment as a kind of movable theater in itself. Clothes seemed
full of magic potential—infinitely transformable tools for self-expression.

The next film I was shown, *Fiddler on the Roof*, expanded my love of witches
into one of ghosts and pearls. My father was sure to remind me that my great-
grandma Goldie, Dina's mom, was related to Sholem Aleichem, the author who
wrote the short stories that the musical was based on. Watching with my father
meant being given a running historical commentary, as he explained "pogroms,"
"the Pale of Settlement," "diaspora," and so on through the context of family
stories.

57

My favorite character was Fruma Sarah—the shrieking ghost who steals the show with a two-minute solo toward the end of act 1. Like the Wicked Witch from *Oz*, Fruma Sarah flies through the skies screaming about a clothing-and-accessories-related crisis: "How can you let your daughter take my place? Live in my house? Carry my keys? And wear my clothes? Pearls? How?"

She turns out to be just a fiction—an excuse invented by Tevye to get his daughter out of an arranged marriage—but she still gets her wishes granted. Although I might have initially come to learn about my Jewish cultural history, I stayed for the witchy ghost getting her way vis-à-vis a necklace.

I asked my dad if I could sit on his shoulders and wear an extra-long nightgown that fell over his face, so that I, too, could jump from my grave and fly through the skies like Fruma Sarah. I lip-synced to my parents' cassette tape of the show, whispering the words under my breath, like I still do when I lip-sync, as if reciting a witch's incantation. Of course, it wasn't just the chance to dress up that I loved; it was the feeling of magical transformation into a supernatural diva, the channeling of cosmic femme powers through the clothes themselves. Like the witches and ghosts and grandmas before me, I came to understand that some powers and freedoms must be expressed through one's own appearance. By dressing myself up, collecting a trove of different looks and costumes, I hoped I could take my life into my own hands.

❀ ❀ ❀ ❀

Fashion to most people is all about looking "good"—I've never cared much about that. For me, clothes are merely tools to dress up and transform myself. To this day, fashion and costume are a little indistinguishable to me. And perhaps that's as it should be. If you are truly inhabiting your characters, nothing is a costume—everything is fashion. Or is it the opposite? If "all the world's a stage," than everything in life is really a costume. Always wanting to look dramatic even as a kid, I begged to wear costume pieces to school. (My mom refused.)

Ever the thoughtful hippies, my parents purposefully tried to avoid dressing me in overly gendered colors. Pink and blue were off the table—instead they chose green, yellow, and periwinkle. When I started picking out my own clothes (from the 1995 L.L.Bean and JCPenney catalogs), I went bold: all black with bright socks, red from head to toe, banded ankles on every pant. To me, fashion was an extension of drama—and I wanted to stand out and express myself.

Now I've come to see that "fashion" isn't so much about expression as it is a vast commercial industry, with a troubling history of injustice and violence. One of the first things that comes to mind is the Triangle Shirtwaist Factory fire, which almost killed my great-grandma Goldie. The 1911 disaster in New York was one of the worst tragedies to befall workers in America's earliest ready-to-wear factories, and helped spur numerous workplace safety reforms and galvanize the first garment workers' unions.

In 1910, my great-grandparents eloped to New York City against their parents' wishes. They were teenagers who didn't speak English but they both found work in the garment industry. Goldie Rabinovich and Sam Gildbord had grown up neighbors and best friends in a shtetl in the Ukrainian part of the Russian Empire. As my father told me while we watched *Fiddler on the Roof*, they faced frequent antisemitic raids carried out by both Russian imperialist and Ukrainian nationalist soldiers—homes destroyed, farms burned, and families killed.

In America, Goldie walked to work from her tenement on Poyl Street (that's how she pronounced "Pearl") every day to the Triangle Shirtwaist Factory in Greenwich Village, where she produced hundreds of shirtwaists a day. Sometimes Goldie lost track of time window-shopping on her walk, entranced by sharply dressed mannequins and elaborate displays of feathered

my great-
grandparents
Goldie & Sam

59

hats and jewels. If she arrived late to the top floor of the factory, she would usually find the steel door to the factory floor locked, so the women inside couldn't take breaks. She had to bang on it hoping someone would hear her over the machines and let her in.

On March 25, 1911, a pile of scraps caught fire on the top floors and the workers—all underpaid Yiddish- and Italian-speaking immigrants, mostly teenage girls—were burned alive inside or jumped to their deaths from the windows. Goldie was supposed to be at work that day, but she had once again arrived late and couldn't get anyone to unlock the door. She turned around and started her long walk back downtown, spending the day worrying about her job—it wasn't the first time she'd lost a day's wages. It wasn't until much later that she heard about what happened that afternoon—the women on fire, steel fire escapes crumpling in the heat, dead bodies in the street.

From what I've heard, Goldie wasn't very proud of her connection to this historic event. To her, this was a story about being so poor that she was subjected to the lowest kind of work, not something to take pride in. In my family, I think it was my dad who always took the most pride in this story, proof of our family's proximity to early labor history, of which he had become a professor. My aunt Deborah, however, frames Goldie's narrow escape from death with a better punch line. (Deborah was my ultimate fashion idol in my childhood years, a CEO who wore colorful power suits with black sheer pantyhose and blond Madonna highlights.)

"No! No! No! She was late because she stopped to buy a dill pickle in Cooper Square! This is a story about snacks!" (I love this version, too.)

Pickle or fashion?

To me, tellingly, this is a story about fashion. The shirtwaist was a symbol of modernity and empowerment in the late Victorian age—a lacy woman's blouse that she could button herself, produced efficiently and cheaply. It was America's first ready-to-wear garment, designed to make money. But at what cost? This story reminds us that behind the scenes, the conditions for the workers who made these garments were dehumanizing. Clothes may have magic in them, but fashion, I learned, is part of an institution—one that, like drama, art, and even sometimes drag, exploits people to make money.

Goldie and Sam stuck around for the first wave of labor protests that were started by the garment workers' union after the fire. After having their first son, Nathan, they decided to return to Russia to reconcile with their families. In hindsight, they probably should have stayed because when they traveled all the way back, their village had been razed and their families had escaped to Harbin, a city in Manchuria. After being waylaid by World War I and the Russian Revolution, they followed suit, traveling to Harbin on the Trans-Siberian Railroad, and later immigrating a second time to America, this time to San Francisco.

By the end of her life, Goldie had forgotten every word of English she knew, and her daughter Dina, who had moved to America at the age of eight, had un-learned all but a few words of Yiddish and Russian. Dina needed her own son's help to translate—my dad was studying Russian in college at the time. She knew some of her mother's stories, but the details were often lost in the language gaps. I think that's why there is such an emphasis on education in my family. Because of my dad's studies, he was able to learn family stories he had never known, weaving an even bigger picture of where we came from.

After Goldie died in the 1980s, Dina and Papa Norman retired from San Francisco to Stockton, California, and opened an art-framing franchise in a mall. They engraved awards and trophies there, too (like the "Best Actor" award she gave me). During my visits, Grandma Dina used to take me to the mall before opening hours to power walk around in matching swishy track suits and headbands. She knew the cute gay Carl's Jr. manager by name and befriended a legion of fellow "mall walkers" with bifocals on chains around their necks. As we walked through the empty mall, she taught me to peek inside every store window, taking in the fashion and deciding what I liked and didn't like.

"This is a very important exercise!" she insisted with a sparkle. "Remember Grandma Goldie's lesson . . . window-shopping can save your life!"

Fashion and gender have so much in common. They are both built on rules and exclusions that change over time. They are both used as measures of normalcy, turning trends into rigid standards. They both require that you spend money to maintain an acceptable appearance. And they both feed off one another in presenting binary sex as the most important division in our society.

It was because of my fashion that I was quickly labeled other: a queer, a freak, a Dracula. Other kids were the most eager to police my clothes. I would often hear: "that's a costume," "purple is a girl's color," "you don't look like a boy," and so on . . . Even at home, my parents warned me that "the way you dress at Grandma Dina's isn't always going to be okay with people. Not everyone will be so accepting." But I didn't let that stop me from taking risks.

People haven't always been so obsessed with categorizing clothing into "menswear" and "womenswear." In high school, I remember seeing drawings of ancient costumes from Crete, considered some of the earliest forms of fashion—belted skirt, cinched waist, long black ringlets of hair, chest fully out. I wish someone would have told me that the men and women dressed almost exactly the same then, further blurring any boundaries. The lack of any visible gender difference might explain why shamans and ancient performers around the world typically relied on only small tokens and gestures to change their gender. The act of drag could be as simple as a braid, a new necklace, a ritual task, because that's all that gender was.

As part of their crackdown on Indigenous spiritual traditions, the early Christian Church tried to make men and women adopt radically distinct styles of dress. (Although they did allow their own priests to keep wearing gowns.)

Gradually, new spheres of "menswear" and "womenswear" took root and spread around the world. Menswear was typically adapted from military uniforms: the trouser, jacket, vest, and hat became standard attire first in warfare and then in men's fashion. Even the "pant" is said to be an invention for soldiers riding horseback. It spread worldwide from central Asia alongside the stirrup and saddle. Womenswear went in the opposite direction, becoming less utilitarian and more restrictive—with tight, highly structured undergarments, fragile embellishments, and fine handiwork. Building gender difference into the designs of garments was performative for everyone, but it also imbued the clothes with even more metaphysical power—a built-in story, a sense of the "forbidden."

One of the first outlets for people to get into drag under early Christianity were the feast days surrounding church holidays. Carnival was one such feast, originating as a decadent celebration before Lent. These were wild celebrations, where, as the tales describe it: the poor dressed as the wealthy and the wealthy dressed in rags, men and women exchanged clothes, laypeople dressed as priests, and so on.

By the sixteenth century, the accompanying liturgical dramas were passed to amateur guilds of actors and they brought even more drag to the stage—organizing folk parades, mock weddings, masked comedies, and more. Carnival goers would elect an "Abbey of Misrule"—a court of amateur drag queens and kings (also called "Mère Folle" in France), who would lead the revelers and stir up chaos for the entire festival. As the scholar Thomas Naogeorgus wrote in the 1500s, "Both men and women chaunge their weede, the men in maydes aray and wanton wenches drest as men, doe trauell by the way." In the 1780s, German author Johann Wolfgang von Goethe described a carnival in Rome, where he saw "young men in the holiday attire of the women of the lowest classes, exposing an open breast and displaying an impudent self-complacency."

But these moments of gender freedom remained confined to temporary carnival spaces only. In daily life, people who dressed in clothes and costumes outside of their birth-assigned genders could be punished by death. Joan of Arc was charged with heresy in the 1400s for claiming to hear the voice of God, encouraging her to cross-dress and lead a revolution. The invading British troops feared her gender expression so much that they forced her to renounce men's clothing before sending her to prison and burning her at the stake, where they displayed her naked body to onlookers who wanted to see her genitals.

Others were put on trial, their lives transformed into the latest scandals. This was the case with fourteenth-century trans sex worker Eleanor Rykener in London and seventeenth-century intersex servant Thomas Hall in Virginia, both of whom were charged with criminal offenses for dressing outside their birth assignment. While drag costumes on stages could be celebrated as no-strings-attached fun—especially folk drag at carnival—drag in everyday fashion was a life-and-death matter.

People are afraid of those who traverse gender, because it is a clear sign that we are not so easily bound by rules. After all, drag has inspired political revolutions alongside the fashion ones. One story from France in 1576 describes a group of drag queens from the Mère Folle society who climbed onto their makeshift stage, exposed the king's Grand Master of Streams and Forests of his many crimes, and got him fired. I wonder if the drag somehow empowered these folk heroes to speak up. Can a small rebellion in our clothes somehow embolden us to stand up to the powerful?

This type of drag uprising was a classic trope of folk justice. In 1631, bands of rebels in Wiltshire, England, called themselves "Lady Skimmington" (a comedic stock character known for beating her husband with a wooden spoon) and dressed in drag to fight against the deforestation, enclosure, and seizure of their lands by the king's court.

Another example are the Welsh peasants who wore dresses and horse-hair wigs in the 1830s and '40s, called each other "Rebecca and her daughters," and attacked tax collectors and toll stations on the British turnpike that restricted free movement for all but the wealthy. The "Rebeccas" lit burning stakes, burned down buildings, and stopped the advancing empire in its tracks . . . all in drag.

Something similar happened on Trinidad in the 1880s, when the British tried to crack down on the Black-run Canboulay Carnival by outlawing drumming (among other restrictions). Some of the revelers were dressed in drag as Dame Lorraine, a pantomime caricature of an angry white plantation woman in a big hat. They picked up branches and sticks and fought back against British police officers. In a moment of poetic justice, these uprisings attracted international attention to Trinidadian culture, which, a few decades later, led to a craze around the carnival's musical invention, the "steelpan drum."

For hundreds of years, carnivals served as a sanctioned release valve where people were allowed to dissolve gender binaries and social structures, connect in new ways, and experience true community among the chaos. For centuries since, revolutionary figures have referenced carnival traditions and their styles of drag to disrupt hierarchies of power, or to voice a little rebellion against conservative and corrupt systems.

People usually stare at me blankly when I say Mikhail Bakhtin is my favorite philosopher, but it was his essays that introduced me to the idea that the carnival may have been the birth of modern culture and consciousness. Bakhtin saw revolutionary potential in the topsy-turvy world of drag, feasts, and bodies that characterized these medieval carnivals. Although the disruptive spirit of carnival was often policed outside the feast's boundaries, Bakhtin argued that its contradictory mix of perspectives and radical humanity was ultimately carried on through the arts.

✿ ✿ ✿ ✿

Drag carried on the traditions of carnival, too. The first "underground gay parties" took place in cities built on the festival grounds, and they were full of drag and gender subversion. By the Victorian age in England, society had created even deeper divides between the two sexes, especially when it came to fashion—which meant that drag became more over-the-top than ever.

Drag has cycled in and out of fashion many times. During the late 1800s and early 1900s, drag grew so popular that performers like Vesta Tilley and Julian Eltinge became international icons. By presenting themselves as straight, they made a living off the exact same thing that openly queer people were being arrested for. Many people today celebrate Julian Eltinge as a drag legend—the first famous female impersonator known by American audiences. Perhaps he was a trail-blazer, but certainly not a rebel. Eltinge capitalized off his popular stage career to create a beauty and makeup empire, selling cold cream and other products to the masses. Vesta Tilley was even more famous in her time as a "male impersonator," supposedly the first to pop-ularize a black-and-white suit with silk details and a top hat, called the "tuxedo." In a fitting reminder that all fashion involves appropriation, *Tucseto* is said to be the Lenape name (which translates to "crooked river") for the land now called Tuxedo Park, New York—a destination for the elite—and the "tuxedo" was developed there with inspirations from around the world—including the Indian-inspired cummerbund and the kimono-inspired silk shawl collar.

By the 1920s, queer parties reached massive popularity for the first time, and newspapers called it the "pansy craze." Prohibition was in full swing, and our parties had illegal booze, jazz, and dancing. Live-singing drag act Karyl Norman billed herself as "The Creole Fashion Plate" and wore handmade gowns constructed by her mother, who toured with her. She headlined the Palace Theater in New York in 1930, be-fore taking up residence at Finocchio's. Other drag queen stars of the era were Ray Bourbon, known for his vulgar comedy drag, and Francis Renault, who played Carnegie Hall more

Julian Eltinge

Vesta Tilley

Karyl Norman

than forty times and even opened his own drag club in Atlantic City, New Jersey (not to mention being admired by a young—and secretly gay—Cary Grant).

But when famed queen of stage and screen Jean Malin died in a freak car accident in 1933, many saw it as the end of an era. Karyl Norman, Ray Bourbon, and Francis Renault struggled to find work in later years, and increasingly faced difficulty from police and law enforcement—shutting down their bars or arresting them for wearing costume on the street. The police criminalized drag through the reimplementation of century-old laws against "masquerade"—originally written to prevent rural farmers from dressing up as Indigenous Americans to evade taxation, but now used to homophobic ends.

Yet despite changing fashions, drag always survives. In Argentina in the 1930s, one of the leading tango stars, Azucena Maizani, performed in a male persona wearing a double-breasted suit or cowboy gear, defiantly butch. In the 1930s and '40s in New York, drag relied on the mafia for protection, and drag king Buddy Kent became a star of the era, performing in mafia-run clubs like the 181 Club as well as in the dive bar circuit. He always claimed that the mob treated him well (rumor had it he once had an affair with the boss's wife). But working within a criminal (or criminalized) system will always come with its limitations and dangers.

Azucena
Maizani

Buddy Kent

By the 1950s, those who had once represented the height of style were held up as representations of its failures. Gladys Bentley was one of the biggest stars of those 1930s Harlem balls. She was known for her signature all-white tuxedo, piano playing, vocal trumpet skills, and hosting skills (she worked at several of the most popular venues throughout the decade). But in the 1950s, during the conservative McCarthy era, Bentley was pressured to renounce her

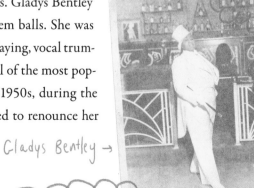

Gladys Bentley →

earlier queer masculine expression as an "imbalance." She appeared in *Ebony* magazine in 1952 with the headline "I Am a Woman Again!" and encouraged readers to take hormones to conform to binary gender and sexuality.

✻ ✻ ✻ ✻

Ultimately drag performers have been exploited for our style more frequently than we have been treated like stars. In the 1960s and '70s, Andy Warhol was selling portraits of unpaid drag queens at top gallery prices. Although superstars like Holly Woodlawn and Candy Darling rocketed to a new kind of fame under his mentorship, Woodlawn would later recall, "Little did I realize that not only would there be no money, but that your star would flicker for two seconds and that was it."

David Bowie likewise didn't credit the drag artists he asked to dance backup for him (Klaus Nomi and Joey Arias). He infused his image and performances with queer codes, creating a look that was viewed as revolutionary only by audiences who didn't know this context. Rock icon Jayne County even accused Bowie of ripping off her performance style and copying "Rebel Rebel" from her "Queenage Baby" (which she sent him as a demo). It seems this essentially happened again later, when her life story and distinctive style were used as the basis for the 2001 musical *Hedwig and the Angry Inch*.

I wish fashionable people, and the fashion and art industries, would just acknowledge their references with a little more transparency. To me, it's even more beautiful to illuminate the forces that shape us, acknowledging the very real people who inspired and assisted what we are able to do. I think there is so much to be celebrated in the connections behind our work—the people, the histories, the cultures. But it seems that being in fashion to a mass audience

Jayne County

requires a detachment from context. Do we always have to hide where our ideas come from?

I prefer to call what I wear my "drag," "costumes," "looks," or just "clothes." I don't want my expressions to be "fashion"—decontextualized with a veneer of elite conformity. Instead, I want to be woven together with all the messy forces and spirits and intentions that have shaped me. For me, clothes are tools to illustrate what's in my head, so as long as I'm happy with what I'm wearing, fuck fashion!

I want my clothes to blur the boundaries of gender. Having both feminine and masculine energy at the drop of a hat (or flick of a skirt) gives you true self-sufficiency in a world still beholden to binary gender. My drag has never been about becoming a woman, or even imitating one . . . it simply frees me from the tired constraints of being a man (or anything else) and lets me be me. As Holly Woodlawn famously put it in the 1970s: "It's not a man or a woman, it's fabulous. When men's fashions start to be more fabulous, I'll use them to dress up."

Even as a kid, I understood drag to be an embodiment of freedom when it came to clothes. I loved what Noxeema Jackson, echoing Woodlawn, tells Chi-Chi Rodriguez in the film *To Wong Foo, Thanks for Everything! Julie Newmar*, "When a gay man has way too much fashion sense for one gender . . . he is a drag queen!" If you truly love fashion, you simply can't play by its rules.

As a teenager I watched *Paris Is Burning*, Jennie Livingston's documentary about the Harlem ballroom scene of the late 1980s, with interviews from figures like Pepper LaBeija, Dorian Corey, and Venus Extravaganza. I was struck by the way drag queens (including many trans women) built their own universes with clothing, specifically outside of the fashion industry. As Corey puts it, "In a ballroom, you can be anything you want. You're not *really* an executive, but you're looking like an executive . . . If I had the opportunity, I could be one. Because I can look like one."

Feminist critic bell hooks argued that these types of drag, with their self-professed ambitions to fit in and "pass," only served

Dorian Corey

to reassure certain audiences that their white upper-middle-class values were somehow universal. But I see it a little differently: The balls themselves didn't center normative whiteness. They celebrated the very queer and Black art of code-switching through clothing and gesture, and the transcendent powers of creation through combination and transformation. Their innovations and styles shaped pop culture from the outside in, and made tangible spaces for future generations to live better lives.

The problem with *Paris Is Burning* for me lies in the documentary itself, which, much like Madonna's "Vogue" before it, captured a community art form without careful research, fueled by the intention of selling its aesthetics to those already in power. Financed, produced, directed, and edited by white filmmakers, the film ended up grossing millions for its producers. The subjects, who weren't originally paid for their appearances at all, eventually protested and won a thirteen-part split of around fifty thousand dollars. Many said they felt exploited.

As I continued my research on drag, I learned that drag artists of the 1990s had derided *To Wong Foo* for similar reasons. The real queens were relegated to extras in the movie (Miss Coco Peru, Joey Arias, Lady Catiria, The Lady Bunny, José Sarria, et al.), and straight actors were cast to play the lead drag queens who, for some reason, never got out of their costumes. It was a surreal idea that might have looked great, but ultimately misrepresented what we do and how we live our lives. Critics wrote the film off as a rushed remake of the Australian hit *The Adventures of Priscilla, Queen of the Desert*, but I honestly still love them both.

To me, drag of all kinds reminds me of the ways that fashion, girded by the binaries, enforced by wealth, power, and hierarchy, will always be insufficient and inaccessible for many people. For the rest of us who find that fashion is not enough, there is something more: drag!

There's nothing new under the sun, but sometimes in the mix of old opposites—success and failure, fashion and the unfashionable, original and copied, witch and beauty, male and female—something brilliant (or at least truly, chaotically human!) reveals itself.

I found my own style in a combination of all the references that resonated for me. Vampires, witches, and drag queens, the acclaimed Ballet Russes–inspired illustrations of Erté, the surrealism of Elsa Schiaparelli, the iconography of Gladys Bentley in a crisp tuxedo. I started by sketching my ideas on paper first. I love costumes that strike you from the second you see them—graphic, bold. I imagine seeing myself very small from a distance and ask myself if it's still legible—an old comic book artist's trick. A good design can grab focus at any scale, in any setting. I love using gloves to transform the entire arm, corsetry and padding to shape my silhouettes, and rewearing and recycling my costumes into new life.

Some people now call me a fashion "inspiration." I say this with terror in my eyes, because I'm still not ready to have people look that closely at me . . . But I'll have to embrace the imperfections because there's just no hiding from them. The thing that really tells me I'm on the right track is when someone copies me. On upward of ten occasions stylists have shown me pictures of myself on mood boards for fashion lines or brands. I've seen what look like knockoffs of my costumes on runways from Gucci to Viktor & Rolf, and on TV shows like *The Masked Singer*, *Legendary*, and even *RuPaul's Drag Race*. One time a Turkish pop singer even copied a series of my photos from Instagram, frame for frame, in her music video. Lady Gaga's team called Diego Montoya and asked if they could borrow three of my looks for her Vegas show. Apparently he admitted, laughing, "I don't own those, Sasha Velour does." But they never called me. (For the record, it would be my greatest joy to rent out costumes to my favorite pop divas!)

A little imitation is a part of everyone's learning process. I've taken inspiration from Gaga and *Drag Race* plenty of times myself. I don't want to be one of those delusional drag queens who think they invented everything. Maybe these stylists didn't see my work at all,

my looks, ↗
2017–2022

and we are all just being visited by the same divine spirits, channeling an extra-terrestrial wavelength that says what colors work well together in a given season. Or maybe their assistants printed out my pictures from Instagram and the designers thought it was just an obscure reference. We all search for inspiration, but we need to honor where things come from and rework our creations enough so that they aren't exact copies. Even if you excel at emulating what other people are doing, eventually we all must break away. It took seeing other people copying me to remind myself that I *must* keep changing, shedding, self-critiquing. Copy all you like, because only I can come with my next great idea.

All fashion involves a little appropriation—you take something you like, you wear it, you restyle it, and you make it your own. Perhaps it is done in celebration of where you saw it first, with credit where credit is due, and storytelling about how it was created . . . but mostly we lose track of the full stories, or never know them to begin with. It's so much easier to focus instead on our own fantasies, looking good, and living our lives. But we would do well to be aware of the systems of power we live in. Power, erasure, and exploitation can be reiterated through who wears what, when, and how. If we don't want to be a part of the problem, we should probably be more thoughful about our wardrobes.

❀ ❀ ❀ ❀

I grew up as newspapers and the internet were starting to appear in color. It was my own little Dorothy moment. In the early 2000s, I was just the right age to fall head over heels in love with pop culture and its new obsession with all things queer. I loved the shows where gay gurus forced "fashion victims" into suburban molds with only the slightest bit of personality left . . . and taught them how to *shop*! I was eager to take part in these fantasies, too, even though I had no money. I would play a game in the mall with my friends where we would pick out one hundred dollars worth of clothes, with no intention of purchasing them, and vote on who had done the best. Dark denim was out, then peasant shirts came and went, now suddenly I needed a rugby top? I met my first boyfriend in the mall, where he worked the tie rack at Express Men.

I came to the realization that I wasn't straight through early millennial pop culture. Luckily, I found a growing gang of intellectual bisexual women who wanted to embrace queer identities with pride: we sang along to *Rent* on car trips, performed reenactments of *Will & Grace* at the school talent show, and rented DVDs of *Queer as Folk* and *But I'm a Cheerleader* to watch in the basement with the volume turned way down.

I mentioned that I thought I might be bisexual to my dad over lunch at the town's TGI Fridays and he took it well. Actually, he had been the one who prodded me to tell him in the first place.

"I notice all your friends are bisexual . . . What are you thinking about your own identity?" (He also made sure to tell me how several young men fell in love with him in the 1970s, but he had to turn them down—never short of confidence, my father!)

Three weeks later my mom asked me if there was anything I wanted to share with *her* about my sexuality. I turned beet red and started sweating.

"Didn't Dad tell you?" This made it worse, and her voice got higher.

"I just want to hear it from you *myself*."

I wasn't ready to put a label on it yet, but I knew that the old plan was out the window. Brat that I was, I blurted out, "Well, Mom . . . I hope you don't have your heart set on me coming home with a wife—let's leave it at that!" I didn't need to worry; she truly had not. She knew that the reason I kept asking if she still had her wedding dress was because I wanted to wear it myself.

My senior year, my high school tried out a "cross-dress spirit day," when students were allowed to wear drag if they wanted to. The girls got really into it, rocking cargo pants and ski hats. A few boys obliged with the odd bra or a plaid skirt over pants. I wore a pale blue silk corset (borrowed from a fellow Jane Austen–loving thespian, I'm sure) and cinched it over acid-washed jeans and a blue Oxford button-down. Pheromones a-poppin', pimples everywhere (despite an Accutane prescription), curly hair down to my eyes, and a big smile with braces. They even took my picture for the school paper. I had never felt happier. The witches had won!

Sasha Steinberg is rocking that corset on Drag Day more than Marian Madame Librarian ever dreamt a boy could.

QUEEN

It all started with a terrible wig. I was twenty-two, living in Poughkeepsie, New York, and renting an attic room in a haunted Victorian mansion for five hundred dollars a month. I had met my then boyfriend at Vassar College and we both stayed in town after graduation competing over who was going to get to study critical theory with Judith Butler once we completed our GREs. It was as annoying as it sounds, and drag was my escape.

I suppose it actually started when I checked out some of Divine's greatest films from the library. I've never been able to convince anyone that *Female Trouble* is fun, easy viewing, but I keep trying. I found a DVD of Charles Busch's camp classic *Die, Mommie, Die!* and wore it out memorizing the 1950s-era song she lip-syncs in a flashback: "Why not me? It's my moment . . ." I torrented comic books with drag characters—*The Invisibles*, *Anarcoma*, *Promethea*. I needed drag and went searching for every form of it.

That year, my first therapist encouraged me to visualize an internal source of strength—something I could cling to even through moments of anxiety. I saw it clearly: not as a person or a name, but as a glowing ice-blue jewel, a set of lips, a pose, a mirror, a phenomenon: the drag queen!

A bit of RuPaul, Divine, and Charles Busch made a "drag queen" in my mind. But ultimately it was a sketch of my own queerness that I couldn't quite see yet in real life. I wondered what would happen if I brought her to life on my body and figured out why this image felt so strong. First, I needed a wig.

It was early summer, and I was wearing a gray polyester suit with a matching tank top, big red glasses, and a poof of curly brown hair. I bought the suit at Goodwill, chopped and hemmed the pants into short shorts, and paired them with gray military boots. I wasn't eating enough at the time, and it all hung off me like a wire hanger, but the outfit had the

makings of something fabulous as I bounced down the hot sidewalk to the wig store I found online.

It was one of several in the same block—a fifteen-plus-year-old Black-owned business with wig heads lined up all the way to the ceiling on three walls and behind the counter, and a center aisle overflowing with hair gel.

There was only one other customer in the shop, a bent-over lady in her sixties with a cane, big glasses, and a fishing hat. The woman behind the counter was wearing her hair long and silky, and she greeted me warmly: "Can I help you, honey?"

I went for it with a soft but clear voice.

"I'm looking for a drag wig. It's my first lacefront and I'm trying to find something flattering."

"I know just what you need," she said without missing a beat. "You've got a long chin. I've a got a long chin, too."

She gestured.

"What we need are soft layers around the face, soft layers around the jaw, a little volume up top. You will love this one . . . try it on! Wig caps cost a dollar."

Bolstered by her act of inclusion, I breathed a sigh of relief.

Following her lead, I used two fingers to carefully grasp the lace of the wig by two points on the temple, then swung it around my head, settling it onto my forehead before shifting the back wefts into place behind my ears. I grasped the jeweled hand mirror and prepared for the worst. But when I got a glimpse, to my surprise, I didn't look so bad after all.

gorgeous!!

She was right, the layers really did do something. Was I . . . pretty? I laughed and did a little hair flick, impulsively, like I'd been waiting my whole life for that moment. I took off the suit jacket and stepped back.

The older customer tapped me on the shoulder with her cane. "My god, you look gorgeous, honey! You look just like Diana Ross!"

"Oh no! I don't at all . . ." I told her. "But thank you so much!"

Even a completely delusional vote of confidence can still lift your spirits. Smiling from ear to ear, my new wig and I made our way back down Main Street, skipping uphill while singing Diana Ross's "The Boss."

Once I got back to the crumbling Victorian house and locked the door, I pulled out the rest of the supplies I'd collected: sale makeup and platform heels from Target, a vintage jumpsuit, then, finally, my new wig.

I took a few selfies, realized that I needed to get the lipstick off my teeth, and decided that the crown of the wig needed a zhuzh (a word I learned from Carson on *Queer Eye* back in the day, which appears to come from Polari, too!). I brushed the bangs, pursed my lips, and took some more photos . . . but something about the wig just still wasn't working for me. I delicately put it back into its fishnet casing and inside the cardboard oval in the bag.

I glimpsed a red and gray scarf that had been tied around my backpack strap and wrapped it around my head. Apparently red lips, big lashes, and a Soviet-worker-looking scarf was the secret beauty I had been waiting for! Try as I might to be a long-haired, natural sexpot, I should have known in my heart that I'd always be more of a constructivist, five-year-plan type of gal. To this day, I still think the wrong wig can confuse the message entirely and ruin a great look.

"Go take that off, you make a horrible drag queen." My then boyfriend came in and interrupted the fantasy. Because I hadn't been a queen in his eyes when we first met, I could never be one. It's not that he didn't like drag. He was the one who spent one hundred and fifty dollars on customized white pleather stripper boots to wear to the campus "Heaven and Hell" party, only to twist his ankle.

"Look at my model walk, though!" I tiptoed down the hallway, to an unimpressed eye roll. He didn't like the idea of me going into the performing arts, because as he said, "Actors are all narcissists." Not wanting to be the problem, I put my drag in a plastic bag in the back of the closet and went back to

Early Drag Photos

watching the TV show he had picked out for us to watch while drinking his favorite wine.

The more I played with the different trappings of gender and costume, the more comfortable I have become with my own "real" self—my body, my queerness that was always a part of me. People may tell you that looking visibly queer is ugly, horrible, strange. Or maybe they will use words that sound more positive, like *fabulous*, *fierce*, or *stunning*, which still let you know: you look like you don't belong. Well, I don't mind not belonging. I can learn to make my own space. I don't want to judge people for what they look like, who they want to become, or where they've been. (Instead we can just judge them for the dumb shit they do.)

Many a homosexual has aspired to be a queen, but it takes a certain determination and majesty to turn that ambition into art. I wasn't quite ready that summer, but queendom was just around the corner. The next step was choosing to go my own way. I broke up with that guy, packed my bags—including my wig—and moved to Russia.

I went to Moscow on a Fulbright fellowship, to document and research contemporary political art. I wanted to learn how free artwork in Russia—street art, mass media, fliers, protests—reflected and shifted cultural beliefs. I didn't exactly tell the US and Russian governments about my dream of documenting and sharing art made by the queer community specifically. But I did make my first public commitment to queerness the week before I left for the trip: I got my ear pierced at Claire's. Right ear, the "gay" one. My mom came with me and helped me pick out a stud earring that wasn't "too gaudy."

While I was in Moscow, I interviewed political activists from the Russian LGBTQ community to help further my research. I even published an article on my findings (although I'm not sure it was any good). None of the activists

I interviewed were particularly interested in making "art." They just wanted to survive. Of course, to my eyes what they were making was art—poetry, films, protests, essays—they just couldn't imagine their work viewed through the lens of galleries, museums, or aesthetics. They couldn't fathom what they were doing was artistic, because art to them was an institution for the rich and straight. I hoped that one day we could change that.

"Veselchaki," 2009

Despite Russia's anti-LGBTQ laws and restrictions, there were gay bars and drag shows all over. While I was there, I even went to the premiere of a blockbuster film about drag (*Veselchaki*) and attended a gay film festival, poetry readings, and even rallies. Russians have told me that their culture is always ahead of the time and behind it at once. I saw this play out before my eyes—not least of all in the way Russian men all had iPhones and were on Grindr before the gays in New York!

CASTA DIVA!

I quickly learned that the most visible queer scenes weren't necessarily representative of queer culture in Russia as a whole: the overall queer community there wasn't just fragmented, they were actively infighting. The activists throwing pride parades were only one small piece of the puzzle, representing a decidedly upper-middle-class group, with certain job securities and privileges that allowed them to take part in global queer culture.

But there was also a parallel network of working-class activists who wanted to create safe spaces for queer people that weren't so public, and organized discreet health and legal services for the community. Some of them looked critically at the upper-middle-class queers for ignoring the needs and concerns of the most vulnerable. They wanted to address safety and health care first, and were concerned that some were too narrowly focused on ideas of visibility and acceptance while people were being beaten to death, or dying without proper housing, or access to HIV care. Both groups had important points and they made different kinds of work to express them. I agreed that we shouldn't let social stigma and fear run our lives or keep us hidden. But it can be genuinely dangerous to be bold when your basic needs aren't being met.

These two disparate groups agreed on one front: their criticism for the wealthiest gays, closeted executives and celebrities in entertainment and media who saw no need for cultural and systemic change. Those who have been treated well under oppression often don't want to change the system. Perhaps they worry that they would be worse off if everyone else had the same freedoms they did, or they don't want their carefully positioned visibility to be compromised by asking the institutions of power to change and include everyone. Although the Russian activists saw America as being far ahead of them in the struggle for gay rights, I realized we had many of the exact same divisions.

Perhaps the biggest misconception about queer culture worldwide is that we are all in agreement, that we have some mass agenda. In reality, we aren't that organized, and we struggle with deep divisions over privilege, race, class, and politics, just like everyone else. A little distance helped me see how fragmented queer politics were in my own life, too.

In the 2000s, the most visible activism in the US focused on the legalization of gay marriage, often at the expense of the battle for gender protections that could keep trans and nonbinary people safe under the law. I felt strongly that antidiscrimination laws around gender expression, paired with legal support for transitions and queer health care reform needed to be our first priorities as LGBTQ activists. I still do. I have always believed that an activism that listens to people of all backgrounds will never put respectability politics over the right for people to work, be safe on the streets, and find housing. I was upset to discover how many in the LGBTQ community still did not want to stand up for this. My growing frustrations over the state of gay activism was its own motivation to put on drag. If I was going to help create a queer intervention, I needed to dress like my full queer self!

I started sketching out catsuits and trench coats, cheap wigs and 1930s hats.

I wanted to dress like a spy, a drag superhero who could bust down the walls of the elite and share those resources with everyone. That felt to me like the true spirit of drag. Like the great drag queens before me, calling myself "queen" was no endorsement of imperialism or the ruling class. *We are all kings and queens!* I wanted to shout. We all deserve to be treated with dignity.

I was reading about the Chevalier d'Éon—a French spy who infiltrated Empress Elizabeth of Russia's court in drag as a ladies' maid to sow discontent about the Habsburg Empire. I identified with her; I often felt like a government spy in ladies' clothes when I was in Russia (once a woman called me "young lady" because I had earmuffs and a long coat on, and when I turned around she literally screamed and ran away). The Chevalier so thoroughly confused people about her gender that when she died, the coroner turned the reveal of her penis into an exciting public event. The doctors still agreed that the body was fairly androgynous in several respects, so the she retained a little nonbinary mystery even after death (may we all be so lucky). But it's another brutal reminder of how queer people are treated, even the royal ones!

Chevalier d'Éon

Still, the wealthiest and best-connected queer people are usually the ones who get away with the most, and certainly are the ones whose stories are most often told. Perhaps that's the saddest takeaway from stories of queer visibility in history: if you want to be openly queer, you have to be rich.

There's Hatshepsut, who wore a fake beard, declared themself the Pharaoh, and ruled over Egypt for more than fifteen years (only to have their name chiseled off monuments by their successor); Henry III of France, in the 1500s, who was rumored to be a "sodomite" and threw

Edward Hyde

extravagant drag parties; Queen Christina of Sweden in the 1600s, who often appeared in menswear, wigs, and heavy makeup and viewed themselves as more nonbinary in gender (to the alarm of many foreign royals); and so on.

I particularly love the story of Edward Hyde, 3rd Earl of Clarendon, who served as governor of New Jersey (1701–08) and New York (1702–08) and was a cousin to England's Queen Anne. Edward walked the ramparts and streets in drag and even opened the state assembly dressed to look like his cousin, sometimes to much applause, bows, and salutations of "Your Majesty." Before Manhattan was a modern city, there was a drag queen walking around in the mud, dressed as the queen, being curtseyed to. Let that sink in!

Although queer people of all backgrounds were undoubtedly pushing the boundaries of gender expression, our surviving historical records reflect mostly those who had resources to preserve and celebrate themselves. The lives of everyone else, by contrast, are frequently only documented in criminal records and moral condemnation.

Maybe that's why for many working-class queer people, drag was an excuse to emulate and become the powerful elite, a chance to experience how the wealthy lived. Being a "queen" held out the possibility of not merely survival but a kind of privileged freedom, too.

Part of the appeal of dressing up in drag was always the possibility of class transformation. Queer people have often adopted faux aristocratic titles as part of their chosen names. For example, in the Molly Houses of 1730s London, a gentleman's servant who went by the name of Princess Seraphina became famous when she took a man to court for picking her up in a bar and stealing her nice clothes at knifepoint. This case was remarkable because Seraphina was the defendant (even though she lost), and the witnesses referred to her as "Your Highness." For them, she really was a kind of royalty, a true cultural leader.

In Paris in the 1860s there was a scandal known as "The Great Sodomy

Company," when some of Napoleon III's "dragoon" soldiers (the cavalry with feather ponytails) were arrested for running a drag brothel where they wore Empress Eugénie's gowns and jewels and rivaled over who was best at "doing the empress."

The term drag *queen* represents this phenomenon, and similar language has been used for drag icons around the world. The *dan* stars of Chinese Kunqu opera were addressed as *xiàng gong*—"Your Excellency." The ruling elite came to the theaters with admiration for the performers, watching shows from a balcony behind a curtain, or paying large sums for sex with the stars.

Proximity to the wealthy or the cultural elite has often been an important means of survival for queer people; becoming somehow "important" has helped keep queer people safe from outright persecution, which has only further reinforced the allure of wealth and status in queer culture as we know it.

In the twentieth century, celebrities (modern-day royalty) have been of similar importance. Drag artists were sometimes able to use their relationships with celebrities to propel themselves into mainstream culture. The comedian known as "Mr. Jerry Walker" or "The Fairy Godmother" released drag soul music in the 1970s through a label backed by Rudy Ray Moore of *Dolemite* fame (who was himself gay).

The Lady Chablis, or "The Grand Empress," was propelled into the spotlight by the book (and movie adaptation of) *Midnight in the Garden of Good and Evil*, becoming the first famous trans performer many people (myself included) had ever seen on the big screen.

Others have gotten close to celebrities by impersonating them. In the 1960s, Josephine Baker formed a friendship with drag queen Lynn Carter—star of the *Jewel Box Revue* who did a vocal impersonation of her and other jazz singers. Baker loved the impression so much, she sent Carter three

Jerry Walker, 1970

The Lady Chablis

Josephine Baker & Lynn Carter in the same gown

taxis filled with her old couture gowns to wear in her act . . . a gift from one drag icon to another! Carter wore them beautifully, restyled with her own signature blond updo.

In the 1980s, Bette Davis was also a fan of her many drag impersonators. Davis supposedly used to visit Finocchio's in San Francisco to see Charles Pierce do his signature impression of her. Legend has it that one night she was stopped at the front door and forced to use the employee entrance because they mistook her for Pierce. In Las Vegas in the 1990s, Frank Marino became a celebrity impersonator and a celebrity in her own right, most famous for doing a Joan Rivers that rivaled the original.

Today, some of the most popular drag artists really do continue to have connections to the top 1 percent of wealth (or to mainstream celebrities). Although I can't deny that utilizing privileges and connections helps us be seen and look our best, it ultimately reinforces a narrow spectrum of who is taken seriously, and what open queerness is expected to look like.

I'm sure the rich and powerful will always have better access to what they need in order to freely express their identities. But can we shake off the normalization of their style? Money is not the only queer look. I want to see the various trappings of wealth be less bound up in what people recognize as good art, drag, or fashion. Queer artists should remember that our best has often come from outside the mainstream. It can be disappointing to see so much reliance on expensive materials, studio production, brand names, and advertising. Our idea of a "queen" should refer to an unstoppable spirit, not just a fashionable veneer.

I myself have felt this pressure. I worried that if I didn't look rich, there was a real chance I would be written off completely. I was taken so much more seriously after I started spending all my money on heavily embellished, custom costumes. It didn't always matter what my performances were like and it didn't matter what I said. The reviews let me know that a homemade look was never going to cut it.

Some of my drag costumes are precious treasures, garments that transport me into a fantasy and inspire me to continue creating. Others, however, were made in a desperate attempt to have something new to wear, something stylish, something flattering, something custom so as to look successful. I regret all the times I spent money to try to give off the trappings of celebrity and wealth. I felt I needed to, and many people unfortunately reinforced that pressure. I wish homemade royalty, beauty and style that challenges our notions of value, was respected more. I can't blame anyone for trying to pass for wealthy . . . but it is a little tacky when it becomes so literal, so essentialist. Though access to beauty and success for drag artists may be multiplying, I'm worried that the definitions of these concepts are becoming more homogeneous, even as new voices enter the mainstream.

At least I'm not so tacky as to reject the title "drag queen." For decades, the implicit connections between drag queens and working-class queer culture influenced many queer artists to turn away from the term. But in working-class spaces, queer people celebrated their lack of institutional and societal support by creating their own forms of royalty and naming their own kinds of elite—king, queen, empress, superstar, etc. This is where the tradition of drag beauty pageants and balls comes from. Molly Houses and fairies' balls would crown a "queen" for the night, and knowing us . . . once the title was given, we kept it forever.

Today's drag pageants are a bit more organized, stemming from the renaissance of drag in the 1960s and '70s. The first drag documentary, *The Queen*, filmed in 1967, captures an early such pageant. In a fitting reminder of the role of celebrity and status in conferring value on queer culture, Andy Warhol appears in a few frames as a judge but his presence is a major hint as to why the film was even made. By the mid-1960s Warhol was putting his stamp on camp, elevating drag queens to their "fifteen minutes of fame" with magazine covers and roles in B movies. To get a connection to Warhol meant bigger opportunities and more visibility.

MISS TAKE

Flawless Sabrina
& Harlow,
1968

Flawless Sabrina built her "Miss All-America Camp Beauty Pageant" into a nationwide network of preliminaries and pageants that at its height employed more than a hundred people. Sabrina was a beloved figure in the community, and continued to serve as a mentor to generations before her death in 2017. She always claimed to love the final minutes of *The Queen*, where Miss Manhattan herself, Crystal LaBeija (who did not place in the finals), turned the cameras back on themselves and called the competition a sham.

Warhol and the judges had crowned a totally inexperienced and somewhat unpolished white queen named Rachel Harlow, who had gotten on a train from Philadelphia that morning and had suspicious connections to the documentary filmmakers. In those iconic minutes of film and drag history, LaBeija decries that Harlow "wasn't looking beautiful tonight! Look at her makeup . . . it's terrible!"

Exasperated with the restrictions and racism of the mixed pageant scene that was bringing real-world power imbalances to the sacred world of drag, Crystal LaBeija focused her attention on reviving an exclusively Black and Brown ball culture in Harlem instead. There she founded the first modern ballroom house, the House of LaBeija. Instead of "queen," she would be called "mother."

Balls and pageants continue to today, and even now, performers move back and forth between the scenes. When we talk about drag traditions, these should be among the most vital because they are largely run and operated by our communities themselves. The first Miss Gay America dates back to 1971 in Arkansas, but it might not have continued past 1975 had one of the winners, Miss Norma Kristie, not bought the pageant herself and started successfully operating and directing it for the next thirty years. Other pageants followed suit, often owned and operated as community-focused businesses run by former contestants.

Miss Continental was founded in 1980, hosted by the

Vineyard Films · Si Litvinoff · MGH Enterprises presents
THE QUEEN
Crystal LaBeija, 1967

Norma Christie

Chilli Pepper & Heather Fontaine

MISS GAY CONTINENTAL USA 1982
HEATHER FONTAINE
436 N. CLARK ST.
CHICAGO, ILL. 60610
(312)

Baton, a bar in Chicago that mostly featured trans performers. At the Connection, a club in Louisville, Kentucky, Entertainer of the Year was founded in 1991, inspired by a one-night-only TV pageant from 1985 called Impersonator of the Year, won by a well-known queen named Naomi Sims (who named herself after the first Black supermodel).

Miss Tiffany Pageant, 1998

Many such traditions existed outside of America, too. One of the most important is Miss Tiffany's Universe, which began in Thailand in the 1990s, featuring all trans contestants. To this day, the winning queens get national exposure, bookings in cabarets, and a cash prize to cover gender-affirming surgeries and more.

My personal favorite "pageant queen" from history is José Sarria, who won San Francisco's first big drag pageant in 1965, and declared herself not merely the queen but the "Absolute Empress," and eventually "The Empress of San Francisco." She went by many drag names in her life, including "The Widow Norton"—the imagined wife to Joshua Norton, a nineteenth-century resident of the city who declared himself "Emperor Norton, Emperor of the United States" and walked around in uniform until he died in the streets in poverty. Sarria was an activist, born to a single mother, a refugee from Colombia. She got her start in the 1950s, working as a waiter at San Francisco's beloved underground gay restaurant, the Black Cat Cafe. There she developed her first drag character and wrote and performed opera parodies under the name "The Nightingale of Montgomery Street," restaging classic works like *Carmen* to be about modern-day queers and sex workers (the police eventually shut down the bar). Sarria believed in the power of the collective to make change, and in 1960, she founded a union of bar workers. In 1961, she became the first out gay person to run for political office in the country (she lost).

José Sarria, 1950s

City & County of
SAN FRANCISCO
City Election,
Tuesday, Nov. 7th

José Sarria's campaign, 1961

Elect

Most importantly, Sarria founded her own drag society that raised money for charity, called the Imperial Court, which to this day redistributes thousands of dollars each year to those in need. *Life* magazine called Sarria "the most notorious homosexual" and she wore those words with pride for the rest of her life—along with her many signature royal jewels! While the rare invitation from the powerful to be seen by larger audiences is a gift indeed, there's something even more groundbreaking about building your own legacy, in conversation with your community, like our Empress did.

Inspired by all the self-made queens of history, I continued my transformation. If my first look had been a Soviet worker with a utopian plan, my second was going to be a campy vampire queen—taking what she needed from the world for herself and her community. When I returned from Russia in 2010 I found myself back at my parents' house in Illinois, shopping at Goodwill for costume pieces and practicing my makeup in the mirror.

I spent a week assembling the ingredients for my big debut: my first time stepping out in public in drag. I laid everything out on my stained jute carpet—a vamp S&M fantasy made of black elastic, a jeweled spider ring, black lipstick, and fishnets. My mom had helped me sew the elastic. "Is this really all you are wearing?" She asked. I carved hip pads with an electric bread knife I found in the basement and bought my first tights and tucking panties. I was ready.

That night, after my parents went to sleep, I covered my eyebrows with glue and powder and put my face into drag (I had to really scrub the powder and foundation remnants out of our shared bathroom afterward).

My high-school friend Kinzie pulled into the driveway. I zipped her into a disco outfit and helped push up her tits to look as artificial as possible as she threw on some lashes. Before we got to the club I gave her a wig to wear, too: that same layered brown wig I took all the way to Russia and back, now back-combed and teased to death (or perfection)!

The local gay bar in Champaign, Illinois, was called Chester Street, or C-Street. It had been a drag haven since the late 1970s. Sundays were their big drag night, and the place was packed to the rafters with the queerest-looking people in town. Heaven.

Of course it was not me but Kinzie who had the balls to tap the local drag legend Miss Ceduxion Carrington on the shoulder and ask with innocent sincerity, "I'm so sorry to bother you but how might an aspiring queen get her start performing in a show such as this?"

I curtseyed to her majesty, and she told me to sign up for a slot in the monthly drag competition the next time I came to town. I rehearsed my number for Kinzie; her husband, Donnie; and their three cats. My performance would be a lip-sync to Julie London's "Why Don't You Do Right" followed by Marina and the Diamonds' "Primadonna."

I performed my heart out. When the lights hit me, I spun into "Miss Sasha" and the audience ate it up! In theater you are supposed to pretend the audience isn't there. In drag you let them worship you, and you throw yourself at them in turn. Every dollar bill made me feel seen, supported, and maybe even truly beautiful for the first time. I won second place, losing out only to a woman drag queen who was gorgeous, naked, and had put in her time with the local community, so it seemed fair. Plus . . . Ceduxion told me I could come get a paid booking whenever I came to town (which I would do twice more before the bar unfortunately closed in 2017). I was well on the way to becoming a drag queen.

"Primadonna," 2012

Is it too much of a cliché to say that drag saved my life? Well it's true. When my weight dropped to 100 pounds on my return from Russia, I pretended not

All I Ever Wanted was the World...

to know why. Doctors took my vitals and found nothing wrong—just a compromised immune system and a weakening heart. I had to face the truth: I had an eating disorder. It's hard to explain why, really, or even put my finger on just one reason. Part of it was that my body never matched up to who I wanted to be—I had been living in a state of anxiety about how I looked since puberty. It took many forms, but restricting food, exercising, and keeping logs of everything I ate became the central coping mechanisms for controlling the uncontrollable. Or so I thought . . .

My mom told me that she went through a rough adolescence, too. When her body started changing, she panicked and developed her own eating disorder. She said she hadn't wanted her breasts to grow because she dreamed of being a ballet dancer and worried that the change in physique would ruin her chances. Instead, she ended up in the hospital. When nearly the same thing happened to me, she was inconsolable. "What did I do wrong?" She asked, but didn't really want the answer. On some level, she must have realized that her own obsessions with healthy eating, counting calories, and studying nutrition labels might not have had the best effect on a little kid. Even people who love you, who are trying to be helpful, can fuck you up, I realized, and sometimes that's out of everyone's control. That's life!

The year I started drag, I also signed myself up for a local group therapy meeting on eating disorders. After the first session I never wanted to go back. I felt deeply uncomfortable talking about something so private with other people, but I decided to give it another chance. After all, I reasoned, what is the purpose of holding on to secrets? It can feel good to abandon control sometimes and trust others.

In the end, I learned more from the other people in session than I ever could have expected. Even though we all had different stories with food, different bodies, different restrictions, we all were struggling with the same standards of beauty and healthiness, and they were often wrapped up in gender roles. We all falsely associated toned thinness with success, status, beauty, and a "normal" presentation of our genders. Such narrow standards are impossible to survive in. What we all needed was a sense of self not tied up in how we looked, with freer notions of gender in particular.

For a long time, I was ashamed to look at pictures of myself from that era, but I've grown to accept them. There's a beauty in the whole journey, and the fact that I have the capability to be such a monster, to be so cruel to myself, is another reason why I needed drag in my life. Drag is an exploration in transforming my body in a healthy and playful way, in treating my self with value and admiration. Drag helped me love myself, whether as worker, queen, or monster (and particularly as all three). Discovering the multitudes within me helps put everything I don't like about myself into context. If being a drag queen has taught me anything, it's that no matter how I look on the outside, whether I'm in jewels, makeup, a wig, a crown, or totally naked, I'm still myself. And there is a kind of peace in that.

My drag represents some of the most vulnerable parts of me—the femininity I sometimes had to hide or fear, the sensitive and emotional sides of myself that I've kept at a distance, the attention-seeking diva desperate to live a big life and be "important," and the integration of them all through therapy. My drag is a journey that has taken me through tough times and grand ones, through catastrophe and heartache and great success. Through drag, I created a fabulousness for myself, not just in my dreams but in real life, to share with others.

I aspired to be all kinds of queen, some changing combination of everything. I didn't think of myself as a "look queen," "glamour queen," "nonbinary queen," or anything like that. I know these terms come from a place of inclusivity, trying to capture all the nuances, rivalries, and dramas with respect for where these styles came from. But when I read about "art drag," "pageant drag," "fashion drag," "Black drag," or "ballroom drag," I can't help but feel that these divisions don't reflect categories that performers want to be boxed into. This is drag, after all, we are supposed to resist classifications, not embody them. Perhaps these distinctions better describe the way we are viewed and commercialized by the mainstream, never allowed to be full artists in our own right, eternally forced to compete within narrow categories for visibility, compensation, and survival. Something that begins as a playful expression of freedom can become surprisingly restrictive or elitist. Most drag performers want to be seen as their own kind of king or queen; it's just a matter of having certain tools and opportunities to make your own path.

Technology helps break apart such boundaries. The internet and social media have shaken up the sphere of the elite, making information, commerce, and influence more accessible to everyone. I certainly learned how to do drag from technology and mass media. The secrets of beauty and how to grab attention are available to everyone, mostly for free. Thanks to the internet and my own determination, I learned how to look like the drag queen I had always been dreaming of, and then some!

But it was ultimately the community of drag—queer people of all backgrounds, friends, heroes, and fans—who taught me how to be a queen. They helped me see that being a queen is really so much more than the look and the attitude. A true drag queen or king isn't just a symbol of grandeur, we are first and foremost a community leader, a grandma, a parent, a teacher. Unlike "real" royalty, we aren't bound by conformity or tradition, so we follow our own internal sense of what is right. But like "real" royalty, we bestow on ourselves the ultimate privilege: to be utterly ourselves, and be celebrated, documented, and remembered as we were—a privilege everyone deserves.

Coming into my full self opened me up to others. I moved to Vermont for grad school in cartooning (more on that later) and met a young actor in a dive bar underneath the decrepit railroad-era hotel where I was living. He was performing in a regional production of *Annie* as Drake. I actually had seen him earlier that day getting coffee—all in red plaid, with his hair up to the high heavens and a loud gay voice—for me, it was love at first sight.

After exchanging numbers in the bar, we went for a dessert date, then looked at stars by the freezing train tracks and joked about how gay people from history probably had sex behind the bushes. We went back to my dire

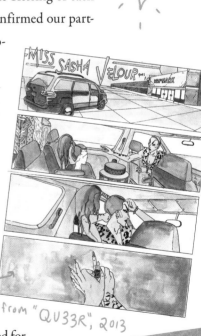

(but well-organized) hotel room with its toilet in the corner and industrial twin bed. I made him a perfect margarita from my mini fridge with ice from down the hall, and we started to kiss. He did, thankfully, refuse to have sex in my twin bed, which is how I woke up the next day, in a cabin in the middle of a snowdrift, in Queechee, Vermont, thirty minutes from my hotel room, cheeks flushed with young love and in bed with the man who would become Johnny Velour.

me and Johnny, 2013

From the beginning, the fact I dabbled in drag didn't bother Johnny. Just the opposite! In fact, he'd done drag dozens of times in productions like *La Cage Aux Folles* and *Cats* (if you count that . . . I know I do); he had twice the experience I had at that point. I didn't know there were gays like that, but I knew it was what I had always dreamed of.

Gradually, he and I enmeshed our lives, and even got the blessing of each other's families without any kind of formal marriage. We confirmed our partnership faggot-style—by staging countless lavish musical productions together.

We became the "Velours" as a duo. In 2013, I was drawing a comic for an anthology called *QU33R* and decided I needed a drag last name. Johnny helped me brainstorm. The comic, eventually titled "Miss Sasha Velour Goes to Wal-Mark," told the true story of the time I shoplifted a pair of dance tights from Walmart, and how much joy it brought me to stuff them into my coat and walk out. Johnny stood in for reference photos of the angry straight people who got transformed into unicorns along the way.

from "QU33R", 2013

We decided on the name together, inspired by a drag film I loved called *Vegas in Space*. There's a very brief scene where a character called Babs Velour is caught red-handed for shoplifting jewelry. The police punish her by calling her mother,

The Velours in "Vegas in Space," 1991

which made sense to me—I came from generations of mothers who knew better than the law. I was obsessed with the name Babs Velour and would find myself just saying it out loud throughout the day. Johnny and I joked that if we ever ended up with a big dog, we'd name her Babs. "Barbra Velour, legally, of course." And I'd be her mother. We realized "Sasha Velour" had a nice ring to it, too. Plus I love that velour is an "imitation" of velvet, cheaper and way more useful than the original. You don't need to be the most precious and expensive version of yourself; instead you can cut corners, eschew normative rules, stretch things out, and aim for more.

my mom, 2014

In 2011, I took my mom to buy her first wig. Right as I began doing drag, my mom was diagnosed with advanced primary peritoneal cancer. She had just turned sixty and I traveled to Illinois to be with her. I was an expert in wigs, or at least that's what I told her. I wanted to help in any way I could, but she mostly just wanted to keep things as normal as possible.

My mother was scared of losing her hair, worried that she'd lose some crucial part of her femininity. Right before chemotherapy, she let me style her hair short and do her makeup for a photo shoot with Kinzie, my friend who was now studying to be a boudoir and portrait photographer. To this day, those are my favorite photos of my mom—I always picture them when thinking of her. Without the long wavy hair she had always had, I could see her beautiful face better. There was nothing to be afraid of! During the first round of chemo after surgery, my mom did start losing her hair ("Like Gollum," she remarked) and finally shaved it all off.

We went to a human hair wig shop in Illinois, one with a special cancer focus (and higher prices). In striking contrast to my experience, my mom hated everything she tried on. She thought they were all intolerably scratchy and tacky. Even though I loved the transformative power of a wig, I knew she had a point. If it's not your style, you shouldn't be forced to wear one. She left the store with a simple detachable bang and some turbans.

Eventually she stopped covering her head altogether. Occasionally she worried it made other people uncomfortable to see her baldness, this visible sign that she had cancer. But she knew she shouldn't have to hide it, so she mostly didn't give a fuck, and embraced being a bald woman.

Today, everyone thinks of me as a "bald queen" in her honor. Ironically, my mom barely got to see that side of my drag—and she always liked my red wigs better than the Dracula looks. But my bald head is still very much a tribute to her. To me, she was always the essence of beauty and power, especially in her tougher moments. When she lost all her hair, she never stopped being glamorous, and continued to live her life. I wanted to channel that energy, too. I love being a bald femme even now, reminding people that having no hair can be gorgeous and normal.

But I still love a good wig. My philosophy is that the best wigs are ones you don't feel you *have* to wear. You should enjoy wearing them and feel great in them. There is something so sublime about how hair can transform your mood, your look, your face, your identity. A wig can make you a queen. But you can create a crown out of other things, too. We have to know how to take off our wigs, all the artificial trappings, and still feel comfortable with ourselves.

I suppose I feel the same way about wigs as I do just about gender: it's a helpful tool for presenting myself, looking fabulous or "normal" on the street, but at home I like taking off as many signifiers as possible and being a little more natural, a little more me.

Today when I call myself a drag "queen," I mean it earnestly and tongue-in-cheek at the same time. Calling myself a queen connects me to a legacy of artists scattered across the world who have dealt with similar forces in many different ways, and who all want to make space for more people to comfortably be themselves. Just like "queerness" itself, the exact role of a queen should be rethought in dialogue with others, looking to the past and present, but ultimately decided on at an individual level, with eyes on the future. The kind of queen I want to be never gate-keeps, but instead opens gates for others, and shows them the way. I ask not to rule at the top alone, but instead among a court of many others, unified in ambition and mutual understanding. As a queen, I say, "We should all be as royal as we want to be." Like gender, drag is really just whatever you can get away with. So call yourself a "queen"! There's strength in agreeing to a single word for ourselves, even though we don't conform to singular ideas about its meaning. We should take pride in the full expanse of our community—queens, kings, and queers, and what we've all been through. We are still here, and we will always find a way forward!

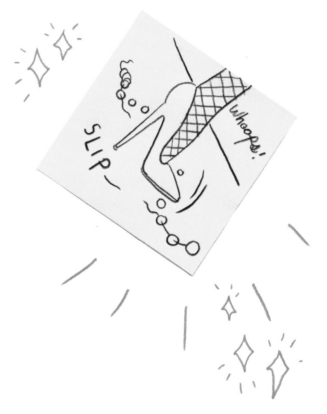

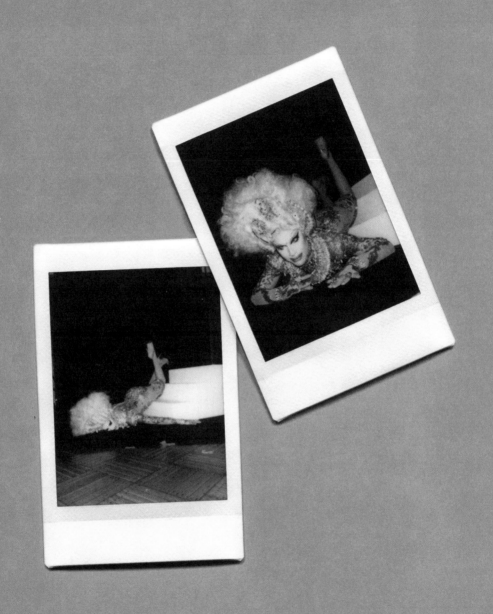

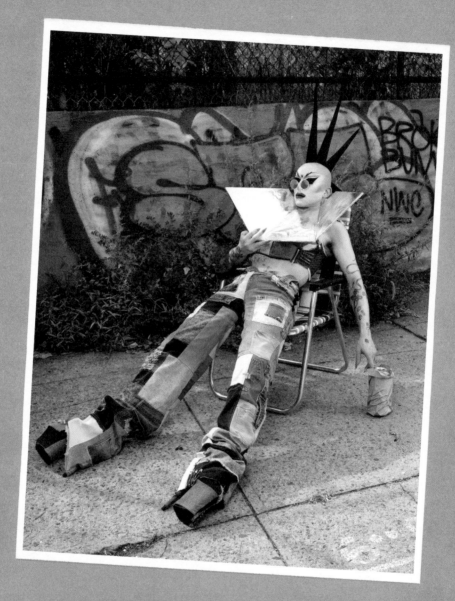

REVOLUTION

I've always heard that a drag queen started the Stonewall riots. I can picture her now, standing on the pavement in stilettos, her long fingernails grasping on to that fateful brick, her lips and lashes screaming for liberation.

Of course, no one can quite agree about what happened at the Stonewall Inn in New York's Greenwich Village in late June 1969. Most say the uprising came from several different directions at once: a punch by a "butch" being brutalized by the police, a group of handcuffed queens trying to escape, a growing, rowdy crowd who hated the bar to begin with. As for the infamous brick? It is probably as fictional as the drag queen who threw it. They might have dug up a few cobblestones from the street corner, but beyond that, most descriptions focus on the broken bottles and the rain of coins.

The most important distinction is the way the term *drag* in the 1960s meant something so different from the professional "female impersonators" or "mimics" at the mafia-run clubs. A "drag queen" meant a nonbinary or trans radical on the street. These were the many gender-nonconforming people who were even discriminated against by their own community, and largely forbidden from entering bars like the Stonewall. This may not be what we think of as drag now, but it is still a vital part of our legacy.

In all respects, the Stonewall, a mafia-owned bar, wasn't the utopia we may envision when we invoke the name now . . . but an imperfect truth can be an even deeper source of pride. As with all things, the way we talk about the uprising today tends to reveal more about who is telling the story than it does about the past. Some versions center the trans people of color, others the working-class gays and lesbians, others the economic pressures and police brutality, others still point to reports that the crowd was mostly young white men. A little simplification might be necessary to tell a good story, but too much reduction can be dangerous. The truth is always more powerful than any fiction, and surely more complex.

In this age of continued police violence, with the constant devaluing of nonbinary and trans lives, of Black and Latinx lives (even among the gay community itself), the story of the Stonewall still seems particularly relevant. In many ways we are still dealing with the same injustices and the same questions that need answering: Who will stand up for nonbinary and trans people? Where do we draw the lines of our community? Who will make space for those who need it most, against all odds? And how will we tell our stories?

One of the first personal accounts of that night I read was from Sylvia Rivera in a 1998 interview with Leslie Feinberg called "I'm Glad I Was at the Stonewall Riots . . ." She describes the 1960s activist culture of those who could not (or did not wish to) pass as straight—many without money and jobs and even homes. Gender-nonconforming sex workers and poor boys of all races sleeping fifteen to a room in a West Village motel. An occasional collegiate who wanted to dance, a butch, or a pack of hairdressers armed with clipping scissors, just in case. These were folks who had marched for Black liberation, women's lib, the peace movement, even the initial waves of gay and lesbian movements of the 1950s and '60s—but had too often been left out later because of how they looked. They were angry, and had every right to be.

They might have hated bars like the Stonewall but they still found a kind of home there. At the Stonewall, you would pay a three-dollar entrance fee at the door and sign your name in the guest book. Well, not a real name—any name would do, to keep up the club's masquerade as a members-only dinner lounge. The club itself was in drag. You got your drink tickets, then passed into the bar. The actual drinks themselves were pricey and watered down. You wouldn't go there for the drinks, the songs from the jukebox, or even the go-go dancers on top of the bar in gold cages. In the bar, surrounded by brilliant outcasts, you came for the community. Only together could you truly experience joy—through the blurring of language, style, and bodies.

The patrons at the Stonewall would take turns making out in the phone booth by the entrance. They'd compete in posing contests to see who could look most like a model from the magazines. They'd reapply cheap ladies perfume—Tabu and Ambush—in the ladies' room, lit with a red lightbulb. They'd sing along to Dionne Warwick's "Trains and Boats and Planes" but substitute it with "fags and dykes and queers." Turns of phrase would catch on and spread throughout the club—and then through the whole city. This was the setting for our revolution, an imperfect community that was still worth fighting for.

According to eyewitnesses, around 1:30 a.m. on Saturday, June 28, 1969, the police tried to shut down the Stonewall Inn. They wanted to capture a mafia henchmen named "The Skull," who had been blackmailing top politicians with proof of their gay affairs. The mafia kept offices on the second story of the building, and were the main targets of the raid. The police weren't concerned about the patrons; they saw them as collateral. After all, they raided the Stonewall every week, so this was nothing new. Here they were back again, arresting anyone in drag like they always did, lining up the bar staff, locking the doors to the club, and this time searching for the mafia (although the Skull escaped into a back alley).

The queers were pissed. They thought the mafia paid off the cops to not raid them on the weekend. Some say there were other contributing factors that made that particular date so special . . . it was an indignantly hot June, Judy Garland had been laid to rest that very afternoon uptown, civil rights was on the news (although almost never about queer people), and according to several eyewitnesses, everybody was tripping on black beauties. The stage was set for chaos.

As the police handcuffed patrons inside the locked club, a crowd gathered outside on Christopher Street. Most eyewitnesses say that something shifted when the prisoners were escorted out from the club to the paddy wagons lined up outside. Some say it was Stormé DeLarverie, the drag king host of the *Jewel Box Revue*, who first resisted arrest and yelled, "Why don't you people do something?!"

Stormé accepted credit for this legendary act of defiance in her later years, when she worked as a bouncer at several of the Village gay and lesbian bars. She was proud to be the "butch who fought back at the Stonewall." But she made a clear distinction, "It was a rebellion, it was an uprising, it was a civil rights disobedience—it wasn't no damn riot." Riots disturb the peace—at the Stonewall, it was the police who had done that.

Sylvia Rivera described how many queer unhoused kids joined the fray, and then people from nearby bars. Sex workers like Jackie Hormona joined in, throwing bottles, coins, paving stones, trash cans, whatever. Zazu Nova, "Queen of Sex," swung a piece of broken metal she ripped off of a sign post. When the police retreated in fear back inside the bar, the crowd started to destroy the bar itself, breaking all the windows and setting it on fire.

As the Stonewall burned, people shouted, "Get the mafia out of our bars!" I take this as a reminder for today: not all rainbow-clad institutions—the businesses where we gather—are worth celebrating . . . and anything that profits off our oppression might be better off burned to the ground.

The story of the Stonewall is not about exceptional individuals, and it is certainly not a narrative of complete "progress," as the struggles are still very much incomplete. It is a story about abandoning civility, getting loud and angry, chaotic and ugly to claim your rights. It is a story about how a protest led by the marginalized can lead to powerful change, in a way that the politics of respectability and representation simply can not.

Unfortunately, it is also a story about Black, Latinx, working-class, and trans lives being continually overlooked and marginalized, even in the act of writing history. I'm glad people know names like Marsha P. Johnson, Sylvia Rivera, and even Stormé DeLarverie. But at the same time, figures like Zazu Nova and Jackie Hormona, who were often named as the actual leaders that night, aren't remembered in the same ways. They didn't give interviews afterward, and history is often made in the telling.

I grew more and more fascinated with the untold histories of this legendary event. I spent months poring through every interview, article, and primary source I could find. I wanted floor plans, photos of the participants, leaflets, and audio recordings. I started to draw a comic inspired by Sylvia's version of the riots, as told first to Leslie Feinberg, then Martin Duberman, and later Eric Marcus in the 1990s. She had seen the details of the riots up close and described them in a theatrical style that was easy to transform into an action adventure, almost like the midcentury comics I imagined her reading growing up. (I took particular inspiration from Tarpé Mills's *Miss Fury*, the first superhero comic written and drawn by a woman, with a hero inspired by the author herself!)

Zazu Nova

Sylvia's was the type of drag that made me want to be a queen myself. She saw her drag, her self, her life's work as the embodiment of revolution through self-expression—the essence of "taking no more of this shit." Following her lead, I began to understand the way that drag brings together queer and trans people from all backgrounds and expressions of gender to do the work, live unashamed lives, and try to make change.

As I drew Sylvia's stories onto the page, dragging them up even further into stylized superhero fantasies, my own ambitions expanded. Although I started researching and drawing the comic-book history to help me see the past more clearly, what I ended up discovering was the possibility within drag (and the act of storytelling itself) to shape and change how people think.

I had a chance to talk to comics legend Howard Cruse, who

TAMMY NOVAK

MISS...

SYLVIA RIVERA

IVAN VALENTIN

Gary

© JASHA, 20

THAT'S IT! NOBODY'S GOING TO FUCK AROUND WITH ME. I AIN'T GOING TO TAKE THIS SHIT.

"Stonewall" comic, 2013-19

drew the groundbreaking gay strip *Wendel*. I learned that he had been at the Stonewall that night, bar hopping as a young student. I asked him what he remembered as a firsthand witness.

"I would say"—he laughed—"if I had known it was going to be a historic night, maybe I wouldn't have taken so much LSD." Even those who witness events firsthand occasionally have to do a little imagination and extrapolation to fill in the missing pieces.

It's hard to ever get a complete picture of history. The only photos we have of the uprising, for example, actually come from later in the week, when stories about the events inspired more riots, more looting, and more celebrations. Photos, like all records, are a privilege, and they aren't quite enough to tell the full story.

After all, prior to the Stonewall, nearly identical uprisings happened in many other gay bars around the country, propelled by Black liberation, antiwar movements, and continued police violence. But they aren't remembered in the same way. Young people rose up at Cooper Do-nuts in Los Angeles in 1959, then the Compton's Cafeteria riot in San Francisco in 1966, the Black Cat Tavern protest in LA in 1967 . . . and there are surely countless protests we don't even know about.

I learned that the reason Stonewall was elevated to such historic importance wasn't just the event itself but what happened afterward, how the story was told. Activists (especially those who had access to press, like the Mattachine Society) immediately started organizing meetings historicizing the "Christopher Street Riots" as the "birth of Gay liberation." They distributed leaflets and zines around the Village, branded with their organization's name.

Ironically, the Mattachine Society had initially responded to the uprising with revulsion, even putting a sign on the Stonewall window that begged people of the

mixed messages from the Mattachine Society, 1969

Village to stop the violence. Up until then, they had been the most visible advocates for "gay liberation." Maybe they were afraid that the complex truth of how people felt, their anger and their refusal to conform, would get in the way of their strategic message that gay people were just like everyone else. Even afterward, Syliva Rivera described the way these early activists overlooked the queer and trans people of color who had fought alongside them. Grassroots resistance has a way of being co-opted by those with the most privilege to advance their own needs.

In 2015, after the US Supreme Court established a right to gay marriage, crowds flocked to today's Stonewall to honor those who, according to them, "had started this fight long ago." I wondered if the true heroes at the Stonewall might not have been able to get excited about the news. They would still be fighting hard to exist, and would likely face discrimination at the gay bars surrounding Sheridan Square, like the Monster and the Stonewall, which still face criticism for their treatment of Black and trans clientele, not to mention the unhoused.

Without liberation for all, the gay rights movement is a sham. Sylvia Rivera famously climbed the stage of the 1973 Christopher Street Liberation Day March (New York City's early pride celebration) and screamed at everyone to "quiet down," calling them a "white middle-class club," and urged them to make space for the incarcerated queer and trans people who desperately needed their help. "Your brothers and sisters are in *jail*!" she screamed.

A conservative lesbian group had tried to restrict drag queens from appearing at this early march. They called themselves the "Lesbian Feminist Liberation," a precursor to today's "gender-critical feminist" or "trans-exclusionary" movement (which still tragically claims a baby's genitals are essential in determining who they are and can be). The group passed out leaflets declaring that drag was misogynistic. That's when Sylvia jumped up onstage and grabbed the mic from Vito Russo (who was hosting the drag show).

Sylvia Rivera

107

Lee Brewster

Marsha P. Johnson

After Sylvia, Lee Brewster, another prominent drag queen who would go on to open her own drag shop in the Meatpacking District, took the mic. She was self-publishing a magazine called *Drag* and had founded the Queens Liberation Front after the Mattachine Society banned drag from their fundraising events. Onstage, Brewster decried the harassment and arrests of drag queens on the street. The crowd grew angrier and angrier, and, according to many eyewitnesses, only calmed down when Bette Midler, who heard the broadcasts on the radio in her apartment, arrived, took the microphone, and began singing "Friends."

Icons like Sylvia Rivera and Marsha P. Johnson are remembered precisely because of the way they told stories and revealed missing truths to make powerful noise for change. That's why I was so surprised to learn that neither of them were likely at the Stonewall uprising on June 28, 1969, at all. Marsha, by all accounts, might have shown up at riots later in the week, but a few eyewitnesses had her confused with Zazu Nova. And as for Sylvia, everyone who was at Stonewall (including Marsha herself) claimed that she spent the weekend passed out in a park and completely missed the uprising. Sylvia's romantic rendition of the riots, which inspired me to become a drag queen, was a complete fiction, a fantasy!

Ah, well! Facts are vital, but the fact that they imagined being there says something, too. Sylvia's and Marsha's alternate histories (which have since become their own kind of canon) may not have been exactly factual, but they were a necessary intervention into the other myths, perpetuated by organizations like the Mattachine Society, that centered on white gay activists. Sylvia's version in particular refused to let queer and trans people, anyone who identified as a drag queen, and especially people of color, be erased. It was that same refusal of erasure that started the uprising, and will inspire uprisings to come.

That's why what matters most are the roles activists like Sylvia, Marsha, and Lee Brewster played afterward in reorienting the conversation. Maybe because they missed out on the uprising, they could see even more clearly the ways they needed to be guardians of its truth.

STAR (Sylvia & Marsha)

They would spend their whole lives fighting for liberation. Marsha and Sylvia seized an East Village apartment to run as their own impromptu shelter and meeting place for queer and trans people with nowhere to go. They called it STAR, in honor of their identities as "street transvestite action revolutionaries." They marched carrying banners with the Gay Liberation Front and with the Young Lords, a leftist Puerto Rican street gang, to stand against police brutality. Picture this: street transvestites and drag queens in leather boots (with a chunky heel), jumpsuits, and feathers, marching together against oppression, while also shaping real practical solutions for local change.

But they still struggled to live comfortable lives. Marsha was murdered in 1992 and the crime is still unsolved. Sylvia spent the final years of her life (she died in 2002) unhoused by the Hudson River, as documented in the most famous photos we have left of her. I know the myths we have about these heroes today are flawed, because they leave out the fact that they were rejected and abandoned in so many ways by the queer community during their lifetimes.

Throughout the 1960s and '70s, many drag queens started grassroots organizations in their communities to support queer and trans people in everyday life. In San Francisco, there was José Sarria's Imperial Court System. In 1979, the Sisters of Perpetual Indulgence was founded as a charity and protest organization, using genderfuck drag and religious imagery to satirize social norms and uplift community on the street.

Sisters of Perpetual Indulgence

In Europe, Coccinelle, the undisputed star of Paris's drag club Madame Arthur (and who made headlines with her "sex change" in Morocco in 1967), founded an activist organization called Devenir Femme ("Becoming Woman") for trans women across the world to exchange resources and information.

In the 1990s, Queer Nation fought back against antigay and anti-trans violence, and in affiliation with ACT UP and the Radical Faeries, helped to demand research and support to fight HIV and AIDS. Queer Nation staged protests with chants like "We're here, we're queer, get used to it!" and supported the first (and only?) drag queen to run for president—Joan Jett Blakk. In the 1990s, Blakk also launched campaigns to be the mayor of Chicago and San Francisco, calling them "camp-pains"—"Putting in the camp, taking out the pain, honey." She called for universal health care, free education, and gender equality, rights we are still fighting for today.

When I first learned about the word *queer* during college—it was always in this kind of activist context. Chicana scholar Gloria Anzaldúa was the first to bring the term to the academy. Her book *Borderlands/La Frontera* was published in San Francisco in 1987 (so you could say the term *queer* and I were born in the same city and year!). Anzaldúa's work was heavily influenced by Indigenous spiritualities that viewed queer expression as something natural and sacred. Later, theorists like Judith Butler and Michael Warner linked these ideas with philosophers Michel Foucault and Simone de Beauvoir, who argued that labels and identities like "straight," "gay," "man," "woman," "male," and "female" hadn't existed continuously over time, and therefore could be viewed as social constructs rather than essential realities. In other words, the fact that expectations for what gender and sex look like have changed generation to generation means that "normal" is meaningless, and can be redefined.

This brought me new personal freedom, too. Queer as an identity (or

Chez André
CABARET · BAR   TANZ
FASANENSTR. 70   TEL. 881 67 85
präsentiert:
COCCINELLE

Coccinelle

JOAN JETT BLAKK
FOR PRESIDENT
Q
I WANT YOU, HONEY!
LICK SLICK WILLIE IN '96!
QUEER NATION PARTY

Joan Jett Blakk
campaign

non-identity) opened up a space for me to exist outside expectations (particularly my internalized ones) about binary sex and gender, and allowed me to play with how I could look and who I could be. For me, being queer meant that I didn't need to fit into binary ideas of sexual attraction or gender. If you are queer, you don't allow body parts to determine how you dress or act. Anzaldúa had modeled how a queer identity could be a form of activism in itself—a purposefully hybrid identity (like "Chicana") that makes space for the very real possibility of existing between several different and contradicting identities.

We need drag to be a part of queer activism because it allows us to imagine (and try on) such alternative realities and identities. One of my favorite writers, Kate Bornstein, wrote in 1994 in *Gender Outlaw*, "I get panicked reactions from audiences when I suggest we eliminate gender as a system; gender defines our desire, and we don't know what to do if we don't have desire." I think drag can sketch out new constellations of desire and desirability, ones that exist without the rules of a binary, and could be carried into real life.

Drag has never been about deception; it's about expressing ourselves without shame, and thinking expansively about others. In drag, we reject our assumptions about how a man or a woman "should" act and instead allow everyone to find their own ways of being.

The critics who cry otherwise aren't trying to inform the public of any real threat when they condemn full visibility and representation of queer and trans people. They certainly aren't worried about child abuse—that is what they are doing by teaching their children to fear themselves at such an early age. The censorship of drag is much less about the imagined sexual dangers of a drag show than the feared dangers of failing to indoctrinate people of all ages with shame around queerness.

Drag is, more than anything, an antidote to fear and shame. Anyone who sees enough queens and king up onstage twirling in costume—acting absurd and authentic before all of society—is bound to develop more empathy, exploration, and tolerance. Unfortunately, tolerance is a threatening trait in the eyes of powerful people who want to stamp out any kind of difference.

This is why drag is revolutionary. Gender and sex are so politicized that doing drag not only asserts the existence of queer expression but also exposes us to the harsh realities of being "other" in society. It changes us, radicalizes us, whether we like it or not. But the drag community also stands up for one another; we entertain and employ ourselves, even when all other institutions turn us away.

If spiteful politicians were ever to drive us from the public libraries and stages, we'd still have our bars. If we were driven from our bars, we would have our parties and our parks, our bodies and lives. Part of drag's history is the fact that we always find ways to transform the world around us as well, to make room for one another. Through drag, we are trying to shape our communities into what we need them to be: built to withstand anything and unafraid to scream for what is right.

In my home growing up, *revolution* was a powerful word—the title for a book, a computer password, the biggest compliment. My dad, Professor Mark Steinberg (or Papa Velour), kicked things off by giving me a copy of *A Very Brief Introduction to Marx* for Chanukah one year. My dad is a brilliant thinker—a historian who pioneered a nonlinear approach that placed people first. He writes history books about the Russian Revolution, connecting themes of class struggle and identity around the world.

To help me understand what he did for work, he acted out the execution of the Romanovs with Legos. I always focused on the wrong details. "You say they were hard to kill because of the jewels sewn into their dresses?" I asked. Then he introduced the notion of unions and worker rights, using my Playmobil set

("These construction workers simply wanted to have a voice!"). Like many brilliant historians, my dad used connections between past and present to set the stage for new understandings.

To briefly turn to history, for example, we could note that the word *revolution* originated as a synonym for *turning*, but it took on the extra meaning of a political or intellectual upheaval after Copernicus published a book called *On the Revolution of the Celestial Spheres*. This book went against the Catholic Church and established that Earth was not the center of the celestial universe, but just one of many planets in a complex system orbiting ("revolving" around) the sun.

In the Copernican sense, a "revolution" always circles back to the realization that an individual's position in the universe is not as central as they might have thought, and in fact, we are always in motion, even without realizing it. This was a radical idea, and the beginning of the scientific revolution, which replaced superstition and spirituality with research. In some ways, this discovery heralded political revolutions as well, because ordinary people began questioning the supposed boundaries of every restrictive system they lived in.

When it comes to revolution and potentiality, I think of Angela Davis, who weaves together traditions of Marxism, feminism, and Black activism. She named the projects of police and prison abolition as our key tasks of "re-envisioning." To her, revolution is not primarily about dismantling and getting rid of, but about building anew—recognizing the failure of institutions from an intersectional viewpoint and actively rethinking the kind of future we want: the social future, the economic future, the political future.

In 2020, Davis praised the queer and trans community for showing people "how to challenge that which has been totally accepted as normal," and acknowledged the central role of Black trans women in leading the fight for liberation for all. Building off feminist thinkers like bell hooks and Audre Lorde, as well as queer leaders like Marsha P. Johnson and Sylvia Rivera, activists then and now continue to challenge the many institutions and legal obstacles surrounding gender, class, and race that still prevent people from having agency over their own bodies.

The status quo does not have to be the be-all and end-all, and our current values are not the only ones that matter. Few know this better than queer people, trans people, and drag queens alike, who throughout history have been cast in the role of the other, asking ourselves and others to shake up our worldviews just so we can exist. Continuing to exist in the face of oppression is revolutionary.

Drag artists don't always want to be activists, we often become so accidentally. Gay bars, balls, and private parties may start as sites of escapist utopia and fantasy, but they can become revolutionary in the face of arrest, violence, and erasure. In Washington, DC, in the 1880s and '90s, William Dorsey Swann organized his own series of balls for queer Black people that were frequently subjected to raids. Swann, who was born into slavery and lived through abolition, called himself the "queen of drag."

When Swann was arrested and convicted on criminal charges for these parties, and accused of running a brothel, the news was published in an act of public "shaming" that was intended to cause difficulty with future employment. Swann submitted a request for a presidential pardon, making him the first American on record to pursue legal and political action to defend queer life.

José Esteban Muñoz, one of New York's most beloved queer theorists, wrote that queer people (particularly queer people of color) *must* devise their own way of making spaces for themselves—and that can be done even from within institutions as they are. By living life outside straight lines, reclaiming radical pasts that were erased, and building toward a future "whose arrival is continuously belated," we can strive to make a fantasy, a "utopia" in the present, in the fucked-up world we've got.

Muñoz took inspiration from the generation of performers in New York of the 1980s and '90s who gave shows at gay bars like the legendary Pyramid Club, and took part in the early Wigstock festival. Kevin Aviance, Lady Bunny, Lypsinka, Tabboo!, Mistress Formika, Justin Vivian Bond, and even RuPaul number among his references.

Most queer philosophy originated in the gay bar and at the drag show; many theorists cite drag as a major inspiration. Jack Halberstam's 1998 book, *Female Masculinity*, another major work of queer theory, cites *Club Casanova* as an inspiration. Called the "world's first weekly drag king showcase," it was formed in 1995 in the East Village as an offshoot of the Wigstock scene by Mo B. Dick and was also immortalized in the documentary *Venus Boyz*.

The Pyramid Club

Mo B. Dick

The most profound transformations we can make are not as individuals but as a community, through our relationships and exchanges with each other. Muñoz believed that individual utopias weren't enough—we need our communities in their full multiplicities to imagine what utopia might look like. Drag continues to make a difference in the fight for queer rights. We have the power as a collective to push the needle for each other and for all the marginalized communities we intersect with. Of course, sometimes the way we fail to "pull it off" can be part of the goal as well. Our utopian fantasies and our ambitions may never become fully realized—they can and should be redefined and edited with every new generation. Our revolution, like ourselves, is an ongoing project that allows for contradiction, failure, and continuous change.

DRAG
NO 4
$2
VOL 1

Lee Brewster's "Drag"

a magazine
about
the Transvestite

I moved to New York with dreams of such a community. Johnny and I rented an apartment in Brooklyn and decorated it with as many pieces of queer art and books as we could find. We dreamed of self-publishing an independent drag magazine, something to follow in the footsteps of a long queer tradition—Lee Brewster's *Drag*, Pudgy Roberts's *Female Mimics*, or Linda Simpson's *My Comrade*, all of which we found excerpts from online (and later collected original copies of). We called ours *Vym Magazine*—which sounded to us like a fantasy pronoun from a different dimension. (I later renamed it *Velour* to be more strategic and self-aggrandizing).

This was a case of using whatever skills and connections we had to make something gorgeous. I had technical skills for making a zine from my day job in a small comic book publishing house, and was starting to meet a network of artists through independent zine fairs. I knew some fellow drag artists from performing at different one-night-only pageants around the city. Johnny handled the "choreography," as he put it, coordinating all the moving pieces with his years of dance (and catering) experience. We put together a fifty-page preview and used that to fundraise eight thousand dollars via Kickstarter to cover the costs of printing and self-distributing the first issue.

From the beginning, we strove to make new connections, pairing artists and contributors who didn't know each other together to create new collaborations: a series of bare photos

MIMICS

EXCLUSIVE PHOTOS

The Golden Age of Female

Drag Zines

MY COMRADE
Premiere Issue!
$1.00
GAY LIB!

Francesca in "Velour"

Veronica Bleaus in "Velour"

embroidered into drag with makeup and costumes, a dadaist manifesto about drag, and many photos and interviews with drag artists around the country—Francesca, K.James, Veronica Bleaus, Kitten N' Lou, and more.

Each day we spent putting the magazine together, Johnny and I learned new things about revolution, utopia, queerness, and drag—sometimes from surprising places. Like the queer theorists I looked up to, I learned more about philosophy from the drag bar than I ever had in college.

K.James in "Velour"

Miss Malice of Switch n' Play emailed me a now-favorite essay on drag by Herbert Muschamp, who wrote for *Vogue* in 1991, "The drag queen enacts the ability of the outsider to create something wonderful out of nothing: a novel out of paper, a painting out of blank canvas, stardom from the body she was born with. Beauty isn't just women's work; breathing new life into culture is the job outsiders have traditionally taken on."

Glace Chase, whom I first saw at the Brooklyn bar Macri Park performing "It Should Have Been Me" in a red dress while tearing out tiny clip-in extensions

Miss Malice

Lady Quesa'

Glace Chase

from her bottle-blond hair, lent me her copy of Laurence Senelick's *The Changing Room*, the only expansive and primary-source-based history of drag I've ever seen.

Another of my drag sisters, Lady Quesa'Dilla, actually studied performance theory with Muñoz himself. We had already bonded over our love of queer theory by the time she revealed the news and I think I nearly dropped a dish of kugel ("Jewish quesadilla," I told her) on the floor with excitement.

I was learning about queer theory and activism through drag, and about drag through comics and zines. *QU33R*, the comic collection that inspired me to choose my last name, introduced me to some comics legends like Jennifer Camper (*Rude Girls and Dangerous Women*), Ivan Velez (*Tales of the Closet*), and Carlo Quispe (*Uranus Comics*). It was Ivan who told me about Lady Catiria (a Bronx drag legend) and got me my first drag gig as an art model for drink-and-draws at the Bronx Museum of the Arts and the Eagle. Carlo took me to Vivika Westwood's (empress of the House of Miyake-Mugler) show in the Bronx, and so on. The way outsiders can create communities, network, and exchange resources is a stunning model of how to make change.

I threw my own little launch party for the first issue of the magazine. It was at a bar in Bushwick called Bizarre, where I had been booked a few times. The show featured some of the contributors, who performed drag numbers and did readings from the issue. Afterward, the venue's owner said he liked the show so much that he wanted me to come back and host a monthly one. Johnny was away working on his second contract for Disney cruise lines and my mother had just died, so it seemed like a perfect time to start a huge distracting project. I decided to call the show *NightGowns* because, as I scrawled on the margins of the first night's lineup, "tonight— nightgowns aren't for sleeping in, they are empowering uni- forms of nocturnal revolution!"

To me, being an editor of a magazine and a host of a drag show shared the same utopian mission. A drag show, like a mag- azine, should be a place where there are no restrictions on the artist, only opportunities—a space for queer people from every background to get their turn in the spotlight and earn a fair split of the profits.

I started taking care of the gay bar like it was my own home. I would go into the club in the afternoon to set up the show, moving tables and chairs, readjusting lights to look more flat- tering, and rehearsing my production numbers. I prepared scripts that attempted to string together personal stories and philosophy with the latest political issues. I would often invite the cast over to dinner the week before the show, to coordinate costumes and create a group number together. During the show, I told the audience to listen up and pay attention, and to my shock, they mostly complied. The effort and preparation I put into the role of host seemed to made a difference, and positive buzz about the show began to spread.

Having studied my history, I knew to harness good press to my advantage. I sent blurbs, posters, and photoshoots for *NightGowns* to all the local papers and sites—*Time Out New York*, *Bedford & Bowery*, the *New York Times*. With satirical self-importance, I pulled the most dramatic quotes about the show for my own advertising—"A show like none other," "the thinking queen's drag show." It worked! By the fifth show, the

posters for "NightGowns"

venue was packed, and performers who hadn't even heard of me a few months before were asking to be booked.

NightGowns is the project that really shaped me into the Sasha Velour I am today. The night of the very first show I wore elf ears, a beaded black gown with marabou tacked on top, velvet opera gloves, and a beret. I felt like one of my drawings come to life.

I opened the show with a performance about messing up. It started with Marilyn Monroe singing "Diamonds Are a Girl's Best Friend" as the tiny burlesque curtain opened in front of me, then seamlessly switched to a recording of a karaoke track so when the audience expected the second verse to start, Marilyn's voice was gone and the music continued. My eyes went into sheer panic mode and I lip-synced a few prerecorded exclamations: "Oh god I forgot the words!" "It's your first show you fucking failure!" I collapsed into a staged puddle of tears and screams. Then the track shifted to Enya's "Only Time" and the audience went wild as I stood up with resolve in my eyes and let the throw of the video projector animate swirling snakes all over my body and costume (illustrations created by artist Ohni Lisle, who had drawn the cover art for the first issue of *Velour*). There really wasn't anything else like it.

The show ran monthly for almost three years. After my return from *Drag Race*, the audience outgrew the bar and we transferred the show to larger theaters, playing to crowds in London and Los Angeles and at New York's Terminal 5. Although those later *NightGowns* were undoubtedly among the best, most important, drag shows I've ever been a part of, my favorite and most revolutionary memories come from the original days in the bar.

One night in the first year of *NightGowns*, my sister Lady Quesa'Dilla burst in the front door in the middle of the final act. She had performed as a guest artist several times in her signature updo and turtleneck gown, but this night she had arrived out of drag and very upset. She pulled me aside after I introduced the next performer and asked me if she could have a moment afterward on the microphone. I really didn't know what she wanted to say, but I believed we could handle whatever she threw down. I handed her the mic.

"Some of us are facing real *hardship*," she began. "I am struggling. Many of us are struggling—and you don't pay attention! Black, Brown, trans, poor, unhoused, undocumented, HIV-positive. I'm losing my home and my job! Ask yourselves: What can you do? What can you do for *me*? Community is how you treat the people who don't look like you. *That* is sisterhood."

She continued speaking—after fifteen minutes I did start gesturing her to give me the show back, but she wasn't done. So I sat my sequined behind on the busted piano and waited. She was absolutely right. Hadn't it been my dream all along to make a space where kings and queens could take the time they needed to tell their stories, to call our community to action, to challenge us? I needed to make room for the perspectives that didn't sound like mine, the people who might not agree with my approach.

The other white queen who was performing that night was so uncomfortable she volunteered to step onstage herself and take the mic away from Quesa, but I didn't let her. So this seven-foot-tall blond queen snatched her husband from the audience and literally walked him downstairs to the basement so they wouldn't have to listen to what Quesa had to say. Of course, later she reappeared to explain over us what a "wonderful lesson" it had been. But it wasn't a "lesson." This was real life, our real community.

In the years since, Quesa has continued to be a leader in the community. She founded the JEM Program, named after José Esteban Muñoz, which created a safe space for queer teens to gather and express themselves. A few years later, her "house" even performed at *NightGowns*! I think Muñoz would be so proud of Quesa, someone who creates space and forges new alliances wherever she goes.

At *NightGowns*, Quesa had called me out on my mistakes, too, and inspired me to rethink what I could do differently with my own space. I began to ask new questions: How could we raise funds for community organizations? How could we create jobs, pathways, tangible change? I didn't know how, but I needed to try.

Revolution is ugly and imperfect and self-critical. Revolution is endless and unrelenting. It turns against those who came before, even as it mythologizes and worships them. Done properly, every revolution turns against itself . . . And we welcome it! Healthy self-critique is part of living a good life. But like all revolutions, change isn't just about tearing down, it's about rebuilding. A real revolution isn't just throwing "bricks"; it's about telling the story after, and building the space to hear it.

CAMP

It was a waking nightmare. Here we were, spring of 2018, eleven months after I was crowned the Season 9 winner of *Drag Race*, and I was having another panic attack in my dressing room, this time underneath the Ace Hotel Theatre in Los Angeles, before *NightGowns*. On the surface I was success personified—a literal crowned queen. But, cliché of all clichés . . . underneath it all, I felt like a total imposter. Being given a platform and an audience overnight, it turns out, while a dream come true, wasn't the best setup for lasting success. Behind the curtain, fame was a spotlight of a different kind, exposing all the problems in the systems I'd set up for myself and illuminating the larger issues within the institutions of entertainment and drag.

My dressing room that night shared a hallway with the hotel's kitchen, and there was a giant shelf of sandwich bread and a fleet of trash cans outside my door. To this day, I still associate the sinking realization that my life is a lie with the distinctly chemical smell of presliced white bread and the sound of cans rattling into the garbage. I put on my red glitter lips and black lashes, and pressed "onward and upward" . . . or just further into my downward spiral. Documentary and press cameras were waiting outside. It took me just a second to powder my nose, Q-tip clean my nostrils, spray on perfume, and slap on a smize (by wiggling my ears backward and pretending to have a sexy secret).

oh no!

I did have a secret, but it wasn't sexy. That morning, I looked at my bank accounts on my phone and discovered that my credit cards were a hundred thousand dollars in the red and counting. My small projects had snowballed into over-budget disasters, my manager hadn't paid me in six months, and my prize check from *Drag Race* was still "lost in the mail." Johnny and I needed to write checks for the entire cast of *NightGowns* that night, but the theater wouldn't pay us our share of ticket sales for months. The job itself was stressful, but my mismanagement and inexperience seemed to be making it impossible.

"Everything will be fine," I told myself, painting on a smile by upturning the corners of my red lips. If I could just sell fifty thousand dollars' worth of T-shirts, I would be on the right track. I swanned out into the bread hallway while popping in an Altoid, batting my lashes, and gliding toward the steel staircase up to the stage, where the other performers had assembled.

"Hello, darlings . . . welcome to another moment of our exciting lives!" I faked it as best I could, giving pep talks and passionate hugs. As host, it was my job to set the tone. Thankfully, I loved doing it, and being encouraging to others always helps improve my own outlook.

I felt embarrassed by the mainstream success, even though I believed I needed it to survive, or at least to make it as an artist. The world is filled with talented people who are just as deserving as I am. Success isn't based on who is really doing the best; it's a reflection of who the most powerful choose to include. The more I thought about it, the more discouragingly circular it seemed. The magic of "fame" was wearing off in the bright lights, but I couldn't let it go.

To avoid becoming an "influencer," I set out on a mission to distribute the bulk of my earnings to the community by creating art and putting on shows. As it turns out, I did such a good job that I spent way *more* than I earned! We self-published the third issue of *Velour Magazine* and collected it into a hardcover art book that we sold on my web store. We expanded *NightGowns* into a world-quality showcase, hiring a full crew, paying an equal salary for the cast, even flying performers to new cities. In order to honor the activist mission of drag, I started raffling off art and costumes onstage to raise money for queer organizations like the Sylvia Rivera Law Project, Queer Detainee Empowerment Project, and Princess Janae Place.

As many have experienced, the work that was paying the bills wasn't what I was most passionate about. I wanted to be home, developing community-driven shows and honing my own drag artistry. But I needed to pay for it, so I spent the first year doing *Drag Race* gigs—circling through gay venues throughout the country, hosting "viewing parties," joining group tours, doing the same numbers, and working in bars where the local talent was underpaid by management. The inequalities in the scene were undeniable. I realized quickly that while *Drag Race* had broken into the mainstream and made life-changing opportunities for some to make (and spend) serious money, it wasn't necessarily advancing the community as a whole. There was much more work to be done, more questions to be raised, more barriers to break through.

But at first I was so overwhelmingly grateful for the chance that I just tried to keep up. I was performing in a new state every day, always at the crack of midnight, then sleeping in the airport, only to wake up and shave my head and face raw all over again. Johnny and I spent every free night packaging orders of the magazine, T-shirts, and enamel pins from our apartment, covering the entire floor of our living space. We had payments and donations to deposit, merchandise to pay for, legal documents we couldn't make sense of, and a seemingly endless string of social expectations. Of course things started slipping through the cracks.

Unfortunately, I was living out the exact *Drag Race* nightmare Bianca Del Rio had warned me of the night she and Bob the Drag Queen unpacked my crown from a giant Tupperware container and slipped it over my head to settle around my neck (because it was too big to be worn without a wig). "Pay your taxes!" she warned. "Don't be like the other girls!" Well, I was months behind on my taxes, and completely broke, too.

I was mostly to blame for this mismanagement, but there were some other factors. The mainstreaming of drag has led to many predatory practices, and opened the floodgates for con artists to leap at the possibility of profit with such a clear lack of artist protections. Like the drag management company I signed up with, who didn't send an earnings report in months, or a single payment from all those completed gigs. Instead, the owner claimed he needed the money to expand his business on our behalf, renting offices, ordering too much merchandise, and hiring new staff every week. He even took out a loan against my store and all the merchandise I had already paid for. It was like this with all his clients.

He was eventually later pressured to pay us back almost in full, but along the way he sued everyone who spoke out against him (even slightly) on social media. I've learned that it's sometimes smarter to keep your mouth shut . . .

Then there was my drag sister, a queen a few years older than me, tall and blond in costume, who volunteered to be the "Chief Operating Officer" of House of Velour and manage our accounts. To be honest, I had always dreamed of having a business partner, and had no choice but to trust my friend's decade of experience working in retail. Something about the way she could break down business in a gentle mansplain-y way made me feel comfortable. As it turns out, you should never trust anyone who claims to have all the answers.

She told me every company needed "creative" and "business" minds. She would be the business mind, handling all the financial aspects of running our operation—earnings, payroll, budgeting, and our complex taxes. In exchange, she asked for seven thousand dollars a month, a flexible schedule so she could stay at home when she wanted, and a 30 percent share of the company . . . This would be the best pairing, she assured me. "I make you more relatable," she insisted. "Otherwise you just seem too serious!" Creative versus business, relatable versus serious. Like all binaries, hers were false.

Looking back, she wasn't even doing a convincing job, but at the time, I was too trusting, too afraid of conflict, and I didn't know how to stand up for myself. "Of course I'm calculating the taxes, darling . . . the budget is in order, that's my job," she'd say, and I would back down. "Everything is coming along, why don't you trust me?! Now I'm mad!"

By the time I finally started piecing things together, it was the Monday morning after that weekend in Los Angeles. With a month left in my "reign," I tried to patch the holes of my shiny queendom. I laid out everything I knew to my friend of three years: the credit card debt, missing earnings, taxes that hadn't been paid, donations that hadn't been made, and her expensive costuming charged to my accounts.

When I get emotional I sound a little cold-hearted, with a faint nervous vibrato that gives away the fire inside: "What have you really been doing all this time? Why did you lie?" She confessed she hadn't been working on anything at all. "It was the biggest mistake of my life," she assured me, promising she could get things back on track and that all she wanted was a second chance. I was relieved. I didn't want to lose my friend. We set a meeting for a week later to check back in and sort it out together.

I never heard from her again. She left the city the day she arrived home, packed up her bags, ghosted her roommates, and took a midnight train to rural Georgia to live in a family friend's garage. I tried to get in touch with her for a month, but she blocked my number. As they say, the show must go on!

"Bad vibes" go hand in hand with blessings, and I was struggling to brush off all the interpersonal bullshit that came with so much "success." Friends of friends I didn't even know were using my name for clout and making up stories. Fans went digging through old tweets to try to cancel me, and even forged a couple of bizarre ones when they couldn't find anything too embarrassing. People wanted more attention, more money, just more of everything. It turned cosmic. My storage unit flooded around my costumes (and the last remaining copies of *Velour Magazine*), and I was having night terrors about lip-syncs, suitcases, and reveals.

One night later that summer, my drag sister (and *santera*) Aja read tarot cards at a gathering with some other queens at my house and gave me a warning. "Some who pretend to support to you are lying to your face. They want what you have, you can't trust them." Another of our sisters, who I later learned had been shit-talking me and spreading rumors for months, politely excused herself. Maybe I *was* cursed. Perhaps I had cursed myself.

It went even further downhill the next year, while I was on tour in Australia for my first one-queen drag show, called *Smoke & Mirrors* (in a tongue-in-cheek nod to the deceptive nature of fame and success). Every night I started feeling a pain in my left butt cheek getting worse . . . At first I thought it was a pulled muscle, but after going to the doctor on my return, I discovered it was a bacterial infection. By the time I caught it, the abscess was inches wide and deep inside my muscle—it had become a fistula, connecting to my insides through an internal tunnel that wasn't supposed to be there.

I ended up needing several surgeries to treat it (each time being passed off to one of my old Jewish surgeon's even older, even more Jewish mentor). I hardly told anyone, even though the surgeries left me incapacitated for months at a time. I couldn't walk or even sit comfortably. We removed the backseats from my rusting minivan so I could lie on my stomach atop blankets and pillows on the way to any gigs or doctor's appointments. I had never heard of a staph infection or a fistula before, so it only fed into my superstition that some rival witch had taken a magic poppet of me and stabbed it between the legs. It turns out they just happen sometimes—set off by a cut from shaving, a hemorrhoid, or even a small skin infection. (Be careful, and take care of your butts!)

Recovery was slow and nonlinear. A couple of times the wound healed over too fast, and I needed an incision to open it up again. Even though I was living out my dream of performing onstage, it was hard not to focus on the painful reality behind the scenes. I was disheartened to not be feeling my fantasies the way I expected. It was easier to make room intellectually for the idea of imperfection, but much harder to accept feeling terrible, the bleeding, and the pain. The joy of drag was somewhat lost; I was uncomfortable, tired, and insecure even on stage. But I also didn't want to disappoint. I didn't want to reveal the truth. I didn't want to show it. I was afraid of letting myself and others down. Drag had become about survival for me, no longer a burst of love and expression.

My life had gone camp. In her famous 1964 essay, Susan Sontag identified the essence of camp as "the spirit of extravagance"—something ambitious and "anti-sentimental." For her, the very best kind of camp was always "naive" or "un-self-aware"—when a person doesn't know they are being exaggerated and artificial, they don't know they are failing to be tasteful. The essay reminds me that we should always be trying our hardest, particularly if what we are doing is ridiculous. Why be bad, when you could be trying to be good and failing like an icon!

But what happens if you discover you've been a disaster without initially realizing it? Maybe that's the true meaning of camp—the conflicting mix of repulsion and pride that comes with knowing your greatest successes have an element of shame, and vice versa. If I was going to keep trying, I needed to accept that a little failure and embarrassment was part of the journey. So I leaned into the failure. I chain-smoked joints and cried while listening to Shirley Bassey, turning to tarot readings and astrology for help. I isolated myself, believing I couldn't trust people, not knowing how to open up. I felt like I couldn't be myself onstage or offstage. I saw ghosts in every corner and was constantly jumping in fright.

I was recovering from my first surgery when the Costume Institute at the Metropolitan Museum of Art announced that that year's Met Gala theme would be "Notes on Camp," in honor of Sontag. As a drag queen, camp felt like it belonged to me. Long before Sontag, the word had been used as a euphemism for *queer* or *gay*. It was originally a bit of an insult, a Polari word we might have used to make fun of one another at London's Molly Houses or in New York's drag balls. *Camping* meant being too visibly gay, too tacky . . . and by giving it a name, we made ourselves feel seen. "She's camping it up, and therefore clearly one of us!" *Camp* was part of the distinctive code invented by queer and trans people to curate our community in secret within ordinary language. It was a tool that helped us replace internalized shame with the joy of laughter and community.

When outsiders started describing gay people as "camp," it took on a different tone, infusing the word with an implication of "otherness." Sontag wanted to argue that camp went beyond literal queer spaces and bodies and was something that everyone had a bit of. By describing camp as universal, she hoped to shake up the binaries of "good taste" and "mainstream." I'd argue that the work had the opposite effect, however. By excluding the queer sources of her ideas, she didn't capture the most basic truths of what the word meant.

Sontag may have known that camp originated in these working-class gay spaces, but she removed it from any specific contexts. She invented a bunch of rules about it, restyling it to appeal to the intellectual crowd that favored abstraction (and who had always scoffed at "campiness"). One writer she references briefly is Christopher Isherwood, who is credited as the first to use *camp* in popular literature, in a 1954 novel called *The World in the Evening*. In it, a gay therapist named Charles gives his own definition of the term to the protagonist: "You thought it meant a swishy little boy with peroxided hair, dressed in a picture hat and a feather boa, pretending to be Marlene Dietrich? Yes, in queer circles, they call that camping. It's all very well in its place, but it's an utterly debased form . . . What I mean by camp is something much more fundamental. You can call the other Low Camp, if you like . . . what I'm talking about is High Camp. High Camp is the whole emotional basis of the ballet, for example, and of course Baroque art." Of course, this character is himself camp—playful and stylized, with a love of the dramatic. (For what it's worth, I find peroxided hair and a swishy Marlene Dietrich performance to be the essence of high art, and think ballet is a bit tacky. It is and should be all a matter of perspective.)

Sontag dismissed Isherwood's description of camp as lazy, but in some ways she sounded exactly like his character Charles, drawing distinctions between "high" and "low" culture even while trying to make connections between them and trying to blast apart binaries all while creating new ones (especially the "expert" cultural critic versus the "naive" masses). I worry that I sometimes sound like them, too, raving about how "drag" should be part of artistic legacies more expansive and ancient than the gay bar, all the while overstating the importance of "art" and neglecting the power of the gay present.

Camp offers a possible reframing of such missteps as part of a vital queer

Pretending to be Marlene Dietrich...

tradition. I wondered if the Met Gala had any of that in mind. But the choice of theme was probably more superficial—an excuse to celebrate the recent "tacky" turn in fashion that was selling well at the time, like the Disney-inspired costumes walking down the Moschino runways. High-fashion tackiness appealed to me in its own way, but I imagined that if I went to the Gala, I'd wear something of my own invention, a garment that could dramatically interrupt the proceedings with the vital queer backstory of the term. After all, camp is so much more than ambitious costumes or loads of feathers. It is about the mental leaps that redeem such tackiness—and "bad taste" itself—recast through a distinctly queer lens as a "brave" act of community-building.

Unfortunately, I didn't receive an invitation to walk the steps of the Met. They did have two *Drag Race* winners walk their pink carpet: the only two who were younger and skinnier than me, as it turns out. Fashion is nothing if not predictable.

Thankfully, I got to do something almost as fulfilling—comment on everyone's fashion for a YouTube review with *Women's Wear Daily*, wearing a Diego Montoya caftan, a giant Christopher John Rogers hat, and Robert Sorrell jewels (beloved by José Sarria and Lypsinka alike)!

*Camping!

I didn't read everyone for filth the way I could have, but I was disappointed at how literal everyone went with the theme. Sontag says a great example of camp is a gown made of feathers—they show one. Sontag says an example of camp is not a dress but a "dress"—they display Virgil Abloh's black minidress with the words "Little Black Dress" running up the side. Sontag says the origins of camp are Versailles, chinoiserie, and artificial ruins—*voila*, here they are! Congratulations, you managed to read, but is it camp?

Perhaps the whole event was most camp in the ways it failed to meaningfully explain why the concept is at all important. The gallery walls claimed that the word comes from the French royal court, where the verb *camper* meant to "put oneself in a bold pose." (There's literally no evidence it comes from that, but go off). Using quotes from Sontag in their own defense, the Met told us that "camp" was something abstract, best understood by aristocrats, fashion designers, and cultural critics. Perhaps the whole event was a performance of elite reframing that was meant to be an act of camp in itself? "To write about camp is to betray it," Sontag wrote proudly, because betraying one's aims in the act of reaching for them is the ultimate camp triumph.

Yet I think camp also requires a certain level of self-awareness—some recognition of its own inevitable failure—to really tap into the distinctive sensibility. Without a little self-critique and the ability to laugh at oneself, every project risks veering into self-important sentimentality. To me, the Met lost this nuance—this self-aware un-self-awareness—when they took Sontag's intellectual leaps and translated them so directly. They reframed her conclusions only in reference to fashion—thereby overstating fashion's importance in shaping world culture, but not in an ironic way.

Maybe camp is at its best when the creators understand that what they are creating is a little flawed or tacky by some measures (including their own), but still see the value in it nonetheless, and insist on pressing forward. For queer people, who face rejection by other people's standards of "normalcy" all the time, this feeling is familiar. It's not surprising we'd be the ones to invent a word for it.

The way no one can agree on what *camp* means might actually be the whole point. Camp is always redefined by whoever uses it—and reveals as much about their own sense of "good" and "bad" taste as it does about any objective phenomenon. Like so many queer terms, camp has flexibility built into it. Queer people are not all the same, and our sensibilities, while shared, are never as monolithic as some might claim.

My life became ever more camp as I grew to see the errors in my thinking. The institutions I had placed my faith in seemed far less magical behind the scenes. All the mainstream seemed to care about were surface gestures and the latest trends. Invites and guest lists were reflections of corporate connections and superficial friendships; media appearances were coordinated to advertise and sell the latest thing; and popular activism was frequently more about self-presentation than tangible change.

Most people, even "important" ones, don't know what they are doing from time to time. And many are desperate to pass the buck and dodge responsibility. Don't fall for the illusion of perfection. This could have felt reassuring: "I'm not the only one who feels like an imposter and wants to start again!" But the realization depressed me even further. "It's all a lie!!!" I scribbled in my notebooks. "Don't trust anyone, even yourself!" In the wake of so much catastrophizing, I needed to take some time to redefine success for myself. Thankfully, I didn't have to do it alone.

It's not confidence alone that makes you succeed in life—it's intention, caring a lot, and taking responsibility for your goals. You can't survive without trusting others, but the people you really need around you, the ones who will stick around, are those courageous enough to also admit they aren't perfect . . . that they, too, have their own things to learn. Sometimes we make mistakes, but no matter what, we clean up and keep going. We should all assume good intentions, and hold each other accountable. We must call out our friend's camp moments and raise a toast to them.

To this day I cling to the people who show up with those intentions. Camp isn't best embodied by our delusional and self-centered moments, but the ones where we learn how to find the humor and absurdity in all things. We dance together, eat a meal together, perform a little spirituality, run naked and scream at the ocean, give each other haircuts, do each other's makeup, try and keep trying, even after we fail. Even if it's only for a season, these are the memories that will last forever.

"Budgets are for straight people," Johnny and I lamented, as we took my first *Drag Race* paycheck and adopted a dog we named Vanya (for "Uncle Vanya" and Ivan the Terrible). Johnny and I had always loved the portrait Catherine the Great had painted of herself in a nightgown walking her Italian greyhound Zemira. The dog had died decades earlier, but Catherine supposedly wanted to be remembered in the happiest moment of her life. She buried her Italian greyhounds in a granite pyramid on the palace grounds. Anything that inspires that much majesty must be something special. Johnny and I vowed to get ourselves a little "iggie" if we ever got the chance, and I'm so glad we did. Vanya has been the most playful, silly, athletic, and gorgeous companion we could ask for. Dogs are so sweet; I love how they try (and fail) so hard to be good—a reminder that earnestness and a lack of self-awareness can have their own charms.

Just because we had to be more fiscally responsible didn't mean we couldn't indulge in the joys of life; we just had to bring it all into balance. Johnny and I started looking for a bigger apartment, farther away but less expensive, and found an unrenovated Victorian house with several floors, a huge backyard, and a wood-paneled basement with a washer and dryer. All within our budget! Had the curse been lifted? Or was this just what good planning could accomplish? On the first day we moved in, we unrolled cheap carpets so Vanya didn't go sliding across the floors when he flew after his squeaky green tennis ball. The whole family was thriving.

Just to be certain, I took a stuffed dog toy of Gollum that Vanya had ripped to shreds, blessed it with herbs, and buried it in the new garden to ward off curses, a protective poppet just in case there was any bad luck still standing in my way. I lit candles and saged the house. I charged my crystals in the full moon, created protection circles, even slept with a bag of magical herbs and jewels under my pillow.

But things always go wrong, at least a little. After the European tour of *Smoke & Mirrors* was cut abruptly short by COVID, I discovered the infection

Vanya

Catherine The Great

in my butt had come back and I had to get surgery again, for the fourth time. I came up with a new grotesque theory that it was the ghost of my mom's cancer, haunting me in revenge for sharing her private stories on television. My attitude grew increasingly chaotic and unhinged again.

Was I being tacky or was it camp? Developing half-serious superstitious about the great beyond? Trying my hardest to be a celebrity while fucking up my own chances? Being screwed over by a tall blond drag queen who skipped town? Wearing thousands of dollars worth of couture in a hallway filled with bread? Trying to reframe it all as camp but then taking issue with the entire framework before I could even get started?

Definitely camp.

When we try to make money off our art, we inevitably lose track of the intentions and community we started with. Gaining mainstream recognition has its clear advantages and it seems pretty harmless on the surface—who doesn't want institutional respect and higher booking rates? Like RuPaul says in her autobiography, "My goal was to get attention however I could." By pushing beyond her queer context into mainstream pop culture, Ru showed the world that we could belong anywhere. But do we really want to be at the center of everything? Do we always need to turn our expressions into profit? Is the search for representation political, egotistical, or both?

On *The Arsenio Hall Show* in 1993, Ru famously quipped, "Every time I bat my eyelash it's a political act . . . I can't change the world, but I can change myself and I can influence the world by what I do . . . the most political thing you can do is when you do your own thing." Ru's drag often champions the belief that being a role model of personal strength and success can help people just through the power of representation alone.

But visibility and respect within the larger entertainment industry rarely uplifts more than one person. Can seeing a few people on the biggest networks, shows, and magazines really create change? Looking

Ru & Arsenio

back at different eras in history, there's always been limited fame for a few queer icons in the spotlight. Nothing lasts, even legends have been quickly forgotten or misremembered.

Representation alone has never fully brought about more radical changes in politics: we may have *Drag Race*, but many in our community are still fighting for basic human rights. Celebrity in the modern era is all about staying relevant, but when you are willing to do anything to retain visibility, attention becomes the mission in itself.

As Ru elaborated in 2017, "Drag challenges the status quo . . . drag says 'I'm a shapeshifter, I do whatever the hell I want at any given time.' And that is very, very political."

It's a powerful idea: the promise that all your problems can be seen as a limit of your own attitudes, and that "accessing your full potential" will set you free. But I do not know if this is very radical. Today's pop culture is full of messages to "put yourself first" and reassurances that freedom can be reached by making your own choices over what to buy and how you look. Drag is sometimes guilty of upholding this myth: that the "enlightened individual" can rise above their context just by willpower and attitude alone, and by doing so, help others be individuals, too.

In truth, nothing is less self-aware than thinking any of us can really be individuals. Queer people should know better. We face real institutional barriers that cannot be so easily toppled by individual determination. That's why we are bound together as a community, whether we accept it or not. No amount of self-determination can give us freedom. We have to keep fighting collectively for it, defining and redefining what it means with those around us, renegotiating the boundaries of those in power again and again, making chaos, and cleaning it up.

But once we achieve some kind of cultural power, how can we stay true to this mission? How do we avoid becoming gatekeepers of similar opportunities for others? In our quests to become as successful as we really do deserve to be, many a drag icon has transformed into a delusional, money-hungry, superficial villain. It's a little tragic, a little hilarious, a little inevitable, and certifiably camp.

Throughout history, what we sometimes call "campy" drag has been the most commercially successful. Campy drag is funny and theatrical, more focused on parody and pastiche than beauty or authenticity. It often leans into clichés like "the housewife," "the aging diva," "the innocent virgin," etc. It can be a little frustrating that so many audiences gravitate to this narrow version of drag. "Failure to be in good taste" isn't all there is to camp, let alone queer art. Is this how people always want to see us: as clowns forever messing up?

Dan Leno

Many of the first mainstream theater performances to put drag on-stage were comedies that used misogynistic drag to signify the ugliness, evilness, or stupidity of characters. The so-called pantomime dame became a beloved comedic trope throughout European theater, with stars like Dan Leno known worldwide. In many cases, these archetypes were centuries old—stock characters from church dramas and folk comedies. Minstrel shows added blackface to the pantomime "wench" as a way of deameaning Black women. These shows were some of the most popular entertainment across all colonial continents at a certain point, purposefully reducing characters to exaggerated physical features and racist gestures. All mainstream American comedy was blackface at a certain point, and drag was regrettably part of that.

By the 1850s, drag minstrel performers were supposedly trying to do different things within the form. Black actors started to be cast in the roles, and they did away with the racist makeup and gestures, making the drag characters beautiful. By the late 1800s, female and male impersonator shows briefly replaced minstrel shows as the most popular forms of theater.

Annie Hindle

Ella Wesner

Among the first internationally popular male impersonators in the 1860s was Annie Hindle, who sang songs in military drag. She lived a very queer life, at one point marrying a minstrel drag queen, and at another time passing as a man to marry her girlfriend. The next famous drag king, Ella Wesner, rose *All About Eve*–style as Hindle's dresser. To distinguish herself, she started doing lightning-fast costume reveals, switching between genders at the pull of a cord.

While ugliness wasn't the goal anymore, the focus was often placed on the explicit strangeness of the performers' appearances, and encouraging audiences to guess the performers' "real" sexes. There was the Creole stunt rider Mademoiselle Ella Zoyara, for example, who appeared as an equestrian performer in an American traveling circus for fifteen years and across three continents in the mid-1800s with the billing "Is she a boy or a girl?" Or the acrobat Lulu, who appeared at London's Holborn Amphitheatre in 1870 and was "unmasked as a boy" by the papers a few years later, to great excitement and much advertisement.

Ella Zoyara

A hundred years before RuPaul, Julian Eltinge prefigured the commercialization of the drag superstar. Young progressive women of the early 1900s flocked into New York theaters to see his shows and Eltinge sold them cold cream, liquid makeup, and powder, championing beauty, perseverance, and industriousness for all genders—while raking in a fortune. Capitalism dressed in drag as revolution.

My favorite vaudeville star was the most truly camp in spirit, but remains one of the least known: Bert Savoy. In the 1910s and '20s, Savoy fine-tuned a character that is still popular to this day: the over-the-top diva, drinking cocktails on the piano, accompanied by a flaming gent who sings along (her creative partner, Jay Brennan). Savoy popularized the expressions "You slay me" and "You don't know the half of it" and offstage used female pronouns with his friends, embracing a queer identity.

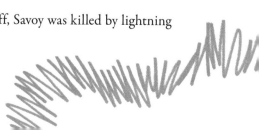

Julian Eltinge's cold cream advertisement

Tragically, just as her career was taking off, Savoy was killed by lightning

on a beach on Long Island. Her last words were supposedly, "Mercy, ain't Miss God cutting up something awful?" An admirer of Savoy's named Mae West took up her mantle (or perhaps, feather boa), carrying on this same style of routine and further popularizing it in the mainstream. At the time, it was perhaps even more dangerous for West as a woman to perform such sexual and explicitly queer material. She was arrested and convicted of obscenity and many of her plays were shut down, including her 1927 play *The Drag*, about the famous subcultures where she got her inspiration.

Camp routines continued to be popular throughout the twentieth century. In the 1960s, Pudgy Roberts toured in burlesque shows with a drag comedy act that revealed to a comedic nude illusion. In the '70s, a queen named Foo Foo Lammar opened a comedy drag nightclub that attracted celebrities and earned her a title from the British Empire.

Although at first look these shows may have appealed to superficial tastes for queer comedy, they were community operations nonetheless. Shows like these raised money for LGBTQ charities, created space for people to find employment, and connected with other queer communities across the world through letters, tours, and self-published magazines (Pudgy Roberts created one called *Female Mimics*).

But not all popular drag acts were the same. Some, like Dame Edna, Flip Wilson's "Geraldine," or Ukraine's Eurovision song contestant Verka Serduchka have tried to distance themselves from queer culture, and even look down on drag itself. Lily Savage once said she couldn't stand *Drag Race* and that drag to her was about comedy, not "[parading] about going: sashay, shantay." For some, the need to disconnect from queer self-expression might be politically necessary for survival, like Huysuz Virjin, a TV personality in Turkey, who, between 1970 and 2000, brought drag comedic sensibility to a country that wasn't very open to homosexuality or the existence of trans people.

Pudgy Roberts

Foo Foo Lammar

141

Success for drag and openly queer performers through the centuries has always been a double-edged sword. It is not a straightforward task to "represent" for those whose very existence is subject to policing, hatred, violence. And does representation really accomplish anything? Something about drag just makes us want to keep trying.

In spite of all of this, I still wanted to be in the spotlight. Even after seeing how shallow or dangerous it could all be, how little celebrity accomplished, how backward it was, I found myself willing to take part. Perhaps it was all a naive and ambitious hope that my drag could be written into history. As a kid, I always dreamed of showing the whole world what I could do. I thought being seen by many people would bring me freedom to be my full self. In some ways it turned out to be true. But every new opportunity comes with new responsibilities, too, new tests and challenges.

Even as success boosted my ego, it was constantly humbling to learn how little I understood about my art and community, how much more there was to do, how easily I could go wrong. Maybe my work would never be perfect . . . but if it embraced the contradictions and missteps and kept trying, it would be enough, or at least it could be camp.

The real magic I needed at that point was a new perspective. I needed to understand that there was something gorgeous about messing up, a kind of inspiration to be taken from disaster. Camp reminded me that a little difficulty—external or internal, self-aware or naive (or both)—is human. Failed ambition is not enough—we need laughter and some creative reframing to transform it into art.

I began imagining an entire show where the audience didn't know what was planned and what was real: the audio crashes, cue cards are dropped, the curtain falls, the theater burns down, the star collapses. I've never really been a fan of one-woman shows, but *that*, I thought, could be something worth watching!

I researched the magic and vaudeville shows that pervaded popular culture during the turn of the century, around the same time as the first gender illusionists. Magicians would conjure their demons and face death night after night, entertaining audiences with ever-shifting boundaries of what is real. But as I researched further, I became less interested in the idea of actually fooling the audience. It should be an illusion, yes, but the kind of illusion that pulls back the curtain on itself. That's more in the tradition of drag. When the audience is dazzled, it's not because they are confused about what's real, but because it doesn't matter any more.

I might have first called the show *Smoke & Mirrors* to honor the act of illusion making, but the biggest reveal of the show was always the imperfect human behind it all. Ironically, the first tour of the show had been booked by the manager who screwed over all his clients, and I was sick from the infection through almost every performance. As I rewrote, fine-tuned, and reworked the show, I slowly incorporated all my real world insecurities, failures, and dramas into it. The show became my first huge independent success, playing to nearly a hundred thousand people in twenty-one countries around the world! "Smoke & Mirrors," 2022 I can't say the process was a dream come true, but it was grueling and unforgettable and that's more my style anyway.

When I performed *Smoke & Mirrors* in Indiana, the local chapter of the Sisters of Perpetual Indulgence showed up in full regalia, fans a-clacking, and took me out to dinner at their favorite strip mall Thai restaurant. They blessed me with a glitter bath and a prayer circle outside in the parking lot. This was the kind of spirituality I could believe in, a genderfuck society of queer do-gooders who distribute condoms, protest for gay rights, and provide

a blessing from
← Sister Rei Ki Kiki

143

food for the unhoused—if there's anything sacred in this world, it is that. What could be better than loving yourself (even though you know how terrible you can be) and aspiring to love others purely, too, while spreading queer justice and healing for all?

Even though drag dabbles in perfection, it's the fact that we are still humans underneath—and the beautiful possibility of genuine unplanned imperfection—that makes this such empowering art. I want my drag to celebrate the way that human beings are contradictory. We reach for the stars and then panic at the last minute. We promise to support each other, and then get jealous and self-destructive. We bring revolution, then police it, or offer it up for sale ... We have the best intentions, but we sometimes also make the worst choices.

Because of its nonbinary nature, drag is perfectly set up to capture the imperfections of our world. It's never exactly one thing; it's always many things at once. The biggest reveal is that underneath us is the same mess you see in everyone else. It's not that *everything* is "smoke and mirrors," but all things do have an element of inauthenticity that creeps up on us. Drag reminds us that it's better to be truthful about it from the beginning than to hide for fear of becoming exposed.

Drag is a style of language that translates anything it encounters into a camp tragicomedy—not just onstage, but also in real life. I learned (the hard way) that drag and camp aren't extravagance for extravagance's sake; they are necessary steps into the realm of exaggeration to tell a truth that cuts deeper than what reality could ever show us—that reality is ridiculous, gaudy, and as horrible and beautiful as humanity itself.

Drag is spending lots of money to look like an aristocrat, then stuffing it all in a bag and going on an adventure, or looking like cheap sideshow act and knowing it is the essence of style. Drag is turning something that could hurt you into your own personal drama, and finding beauty (or even a little shameful profit) in it. Drag is allowing yourself just to be yourself, which is to say: as absurd, as fucked-up, as sublime as everyone else.

art.

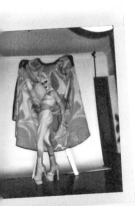

I love bad art. In fact, before I can give any advice about making "good" art, I would like to recall some of my worst failures.

One time at *NightGowns* I performed a lip-sync to "Break Down and Let It All Out" by Nina Simone. My concept was just stomping on the stage, crying, and screaming into a microphone during every musical break. I got so into it, I broke off one of my pink plastic heels. I didn't get a single tip. "Ah well, that worked in my head," I sheepishly acknowledged, which has since become a sometimes catchphrase (even though I wish it wasn't).

Another time, at New York Fashion Week in 2018, I directed and hosted the brand Opening Ceremony's show and completely froze while performing. The audience included my heroes Nicki Minaj, Baz Luhrmann, and Whoopi Goldberg. My armpits were sweating profusely. I dropped the cue cards, forgot what I was saying, and chipped my front tooth pulling the microphone out of its stand. I could taste a piece of tooth in my mouth, and felt the new tiny V-shaped gap between my front teeth.

"Well, if nothing else, this night will be remembered as the time I broke my tooth!"

No one reacted.

"Make some noise for your next performer!" Soft applause. When in doubt, drag queen clichés save the day. I suddenly remembered that my mom's front tooth had been chipped, too—an accident from when she was a little girl. The chip in my tooth is tiny by comparison, but it felt like yet another haunting.

My drag debut in New York had been a bit of a disaster, too. It took place inside an abandoned Brooklyn bathhouse in the middle of winter, where theater troupes from around the city were performing experimental pieces in what used to be a pool, lit with cheap purple footlights. I curated a gallery of six visual artists who sold prints and originals around the periphery of the space and I had blown up some single panels of my comics, too, repackaged as colorful commercial artwork.

I asked if I could add a drag number to the mix, but instead of having me on the main stage, the organizers wanted me to be more "immersive"—I'd pull a few people into a separate, darker space upstairs, *Sleep No More*–style, for a few rounds of barely lit shows. I would have agreed to anything at that point. But the night of the show, fate must have been on my side (or against it), because the venue lost all power upstairs, making it a safety hazard . . . and I ended up doing all my numbers back-to-back on the main stage (with costume changes in plain sight) for the two hundred freezing New Yorkers who packed into the venue on a *Time Out New York* recommendation.

In one number, I became Gollum onstage (to represent the way obligatory heterosexuality makes people monstrously beholden to rings and marriage). In another I died and came back to life as a vampire to the tune of Celine Dion's "It's All Coming Back to Me Now" (and "bled" from my eyes). For my finale I danced passionately (if inexpertly) to a mash-up of Reading Rainbow, Dorian Corey, and Salt-N-Pepa, and collapsed to thunderous applause.

my first NYC show, 2014

Johnny thought I nailed it (even though he was surely biased). "I've lived here a decade, and I've never seen an audience captivated like that!" His belief in me filled me with a newfound pride. I felt powerful as Sasha Velour, all the more so for having turned a near disaster into a triumph.

Sometimes disaster and success are hard to distinguish. The binary of failure and success is flawed because every work of art is some combination of both (and neither). Every artist makes missteps—that's part of a successful process.

It was because of that performance that I got my first booking at Bizarre, the bar that later hosted *NightGowns*. A queen named Madame Vivien V had been in the audience and she gave me her card and an invite to do a number at her show *Bordello*. I created a new performance for it the next month, set to Shirley Bassey's "If You Go Away" where I flipped through thirty different printed-out illustrations and did costume reveals to match. The illustrations told the story of a vampire who, after being rejected by the love of her life, chased him down and took bloody revenge. You know, a classic queer fairy tale. After the show, on Madame Viv's encouragement, I set up shop on a cabaret table and sold the individual pages for ten dollars, cash. The images went home with people and became part of their lives, decorating walls all over Brooklyn, taking on new meanings beyond the performance. Some of those buyers went on to become my first friends in the Brooklyn drag scene; art really can connect people. I considered that performance one of my biggest successes to date—but I still had plenty of notes for myself. I've redrawn the artwork and edited the story every time I've performed that number since. My favorite thing about art is that there is always something to fix.

What is art and why does it matter? Don't judge me, but some of my favorite theories on the subject come from a 1897 essay by Russian writer Leo Tolstoy. Tolstoy had become a grumpy, elderly Christian recluse by the time he wrote it, and devoted most of the essay to making bitingly shady points about the art establishment. He critiqued how self-indulgent, elitist, and profit-driven the arts had become, singling out opera composer Richard Wagner as the worst offender, but even finding fault in his own earlier work, including *Anna Karenina*.

Tolstoy's explanations for why art is important centered on its religious potential. He argued that art has the power to translate emotional experiences from one's interior outward to the community, which brings people together toward new common understanding (which for him was all about Jesus). There is something about this that I love. My own translation of the text reads, "a real work of art destroys, in the consciousness of the receiver, the separation between themself and the artist . . . between themself and all whose minds receive this work of art. The great attractive force of art lies in this act of freeing our personality from its separation and isolation, of uniting it with others." When art captures emotion or illuminates fragility, it speaks to the human spirit inside all of us, and inspires deeper understanding between us.

Art is a task of translation, between self and others, internal and external, abstract and real. As Tolstoy later puts it, "The purpose of art is to translate, from the realm of intellect to the realm of a truth that you can feel, the fact that people's well-being lies in being united among themselves and in establishing, in place of the violence that now reigns, a kingdom of love—the highest aim of human life." Like all translations, the meaning of art is never fixed because people come with such different experiences and values. The "best" art captures this.

Art is necessary for our personal survival because it brings us into a community. In doing so, by cultivating shared experiences on common ground, it also illuminates a more humanistic path forward. To Tolstoy, this was "God" . . . to me, it's drag.

Art should be accessible to all people. Drag is art. Books are art. Painting is art, dance is art, costumes are art, gardening is art. Anything can be art if you do it with expression. Art is in the eye of the artist, the eye of the audience, the eye of the critic. Bad art is still art. Of course, "good" and "bad," "success" and "failure," are completely subjective, bound to shift based on who's looking at them, and in what context.

Tolstoy stated in his essay that he preferred only the most "naive" forms of art—the songs of an amateur folk chorus, for example—where the artist isn't trying hard to be a "great artist" but is instead focused on completing something beautiful, joyful, and meaningful to them or their communities.

The art world, as he was right to criticize, usually does the opposite—they take the goal of finding "great art" with the utmost seriousness. In order to determine what that means, they establish categories to judge the art by, give certain institutions the power to make those judgments, and fund only what backs their judgments up. It could never be anything but absurdly circular.

Indeed, critics, galleries, and museums look for work that reminds them of art that already exists, from people with connections to the same institutions, and with a continued distaste for the art that most people make and enjoy: hobby art, design, fan art, amateur performance, popular dance, comics, poetry, and more. To maintain the illusion that some art is more noteworthy, you always end up making some absurd exclusions.

As great as local and folk arts can be, however, I don't entirely agree with Tolstoy that only the "naive" can make good art. Infusing your work with intention and ambition can be a great thing. I love art that has sincerity, camp, sarcasm, and disaster all mixed into one. Perhaps it's impossible to evaluate "good" or "successful" art in the traditional sense, because these things are so subjective. I wonder if it would be better to evaluate how *transformative* a piece of art is. We could ask, taking a cue from Tolstoy, how much the art has united us together in the appreciation of the timeless: joy, shame, rebellion, love—or pointed us toward a better understanding, a clearer vision of our world (and perhaps a design for the next). Transformative art is an experience, accessible to everyone, that helps us process our world and shift the way we think and interact with one another.

Transformative art follows the imagination. It steps away from the obvious and inspires new options. It encourages the artist and audience to keep open minds, shift their expectations, and continually reexamine the work to keep it relevant. Transformative art gives us hope that, at the very least, we can always be surprised.

It was drag that helped me see once and for all how art could achieve this task. Drag exists in conversation with community, reflecting the world around us and celebrating, stylizing, critiquing, and reinventing it in service of something better. Because of drag's capacity for self-critique and its legacy of revolutionary action, it knows how to revise its own approaches and laugh in the face of its failures. Drag translates emotion between audience and performers—music becomes the heartbeat, visuals make the imaginary real, and dance and speech exaggerate life itself. Drag is able to resonate with people who have no interest in institutional art. But like all forms of art, it is the conversations continued afterward between artists and audiences that truly give the work meaning. I think the best, most transformative work always illuminates the need for this.

Without a response from the audience, even the most ambitious and exciting creative ideas can fall flat. Sometimes the message isn't clear enough, or it doesn't make a lasting transformation; sometimes it fails on a deeper level—regurgitating harmful clichés, silencing or restricting those it depicts, policing what's normal, or even exploiting the people who work on it.

The art of drag makes space for the possibility of these kinds of failure, too. Drag even applauds failure from time to time. Where other forms of art may take complete disaster more to heart, drag is well equipped to chalk it up to just another moment of life. Ours is not an artform for the easily discouraged. But if you keep trying, there will always be another number, another show, another chance to turn your tragedies into a gesture or joke.

Growing up, I always knew that I had no special talent for art. Even as a kid, I felt certain I would never be a poet, painter, or dancer. But I still loved art. I made paintings to decorate my walls. I put on puppet shows. And of course, I continued playing dress-up. Art matched the way I saw the world—visual flashes, emotions, images. I've never had much of an internal monologue, which made linear storytelling almost impossible. I started sketching every day for fun and my early drawings were just messes of lines, but they made me happy.

The first art classes I took were in grade school, and I was immediately labeled as remedial. I didn't mind chaos and would grin widely as I slapped paint everywhere, reveling in accidental abstraction. In a pottery lesson, instead of making a bowl, I tried to make a wig with long flowing hair and bangs, all out of clay. It came out of the oven cracked in two, but at least it looked better than my "dinosaurs," which were just blobs with legs and a few finger holes as eyes.

Out of necessity, I always embraced abstraction over realism (even before I knew a thing about art). I love modern art because abstraction makes imagination accessible to everyone, even the "less technically precise." I think it's good to see a piece of art and think, "I could do that." When barriers and gatekeeping standards are broken down, art, like society, grows with new voices that can finally take part.

In high school, I turned to drawing out of gay boredom, doodling naked men with big penises wrestling (which I'd then rip out and hide) or a lavish French-chateau dream house with an indoor-outdoor pool and a spiral staircase. Most of my schoolwork got turned in with illustrations of fantasy dresses and tailcoats in the margins.

My formal introduction to comics was through Grandma Jo, who, unlike my erudite parents, made no claims about knowing high art. She always cut out her favorite gag comics from the *Wall Street Journal* and glue them alongside family portraits in her scrapbooks. My mom would roll her eyes at the sexist undertones, which only affirmed that I didn't really understand the jokes. Taking Grandma Jo's lead, I read all the comics in our local newspaper. I loved *Calvin and Hobbes* and *Garfield* but would cut out characters from the more realistic *Prince Valiant* strips to use as actors in my puppet theater. I love art and storytelling that uses many different forms at once. When you put visuals and text and color together it encourages the audience to stay involved, piecing the entire story together for themselves. Comics could look like anything, from gallery art to a scribbly childhood sketch. No matter the aesthetic, all the elements of a comic work together, utilizing multiple genres and forms of expression in service of storytelling and world building.

Multimedia art is ancient. The best-known examples of prehistoric art, after all, are cave paintings about animals, people, and magic told as a sequential narrative! These early artworks would have gone hand in hand with drag rituals, shamans, and healers. Art was seen as a conduit between the sacred and the everyday, and performance brought it all to life.

Comics, like drag, fall between several genres at once—text and art, prehistoric and ultramodern, high art and low art. Perhaps it was this nonbinary nature that made me gravitate to them, and gave me a sense of clarity about how to make something that I would love.

a diary comic, 2011

After I graduated from college, I started drawing a simple comic in my notebook every day. The first was about making coffee; the second was about cutting a grapefruit; the third was about hugging a friend in the subway station. When I ran out of personal experiences I was ready to draw from, I drew from things I was reading about at the time: Sylvia Rivera at Stonewall, Leo Tolstoy, the history of the circus . . .

I decided not to pursue a PhD, going against what I had planned for so long. I wanted to make art, not just write about it anymore. At first my parents were shocked. I told them I had secretly applied and been accepted to the Center for Cartoon Studies in Vermont. I presented them with a practical financial plan. It *did* involve them giving me some of Grandpa Howard's 1980s government bonds for tuition, but I had already lined up a student job to offset my living expenses: kiln operator and

checkout queen at a pottery-painting studio (thank goddess I needed no actual pottery skills)!

My parents were always more the art museum, ballet, and Bach-loving kind . . . so I think comics (and later drag) struck them as a little "lowbrow" at first. But they admitted it did make sense for me. "You've always loved the interdisciplinary," they noted with a little apprehension, most likely thinking about every time I asked my teachers to let me turn a school project into an art piece, a play, or a film. Eventually, like all those who truly love art (and not just the pretense of it), my parents came around to see the power in forms they might have overlooked at first.

Even with their self-professed "delightfully snobby" taste, I still think my parents were the reason I have such a good relationship with making art. They were the ones who encouraged me to talk about and respond to art. They taught me to never be afraid of saying "I don't understand it." They taught me to think about what could be done better, while always finding something to celebrate. At home, I saw them practice their own forms of art for fun: my dad played guitar and led cowboy sing-alongs; my mom made beautiful quilts that decorated our walls. I loved the witchy imagery she sewed in her patterns: houses, crescent moons, stars, trees, and roses—symbols that have stayed with me ever since.

They trusted that I knew my own path best and helped me get myself to cartooning school. It was an act of support that changed my life, because everything I learned about art truly started with comics. Through comics, I learned that our full selves—our references, voices, choices, politics, even our limitations—belong as part of our art. I developed the language to discuss art, frameworks for telling great stories, and the design skills to strategically stage big reveals with simple effects.

The history of modern comics goes back to early newspapers at the turn of the twentieth century. Thanks to printing technology, artists could quickly respond to themes of the times and reach mass audiences of all classes. From the beginning, the lines between the genres were blurry, which many creators used to their advantage, combining different drawing styles, page layouts, and narratives to jump between different forms, and break away from clichés.

It's surprising that comics are still largely overlooked by so many artistic institutions. You might think Roy Lichtenstein would be a counterexample, but it turns out he's a somewhat hated figure among cartoonists—known for enlarging and tracing uncredited comic artists' works to upsell them to the art industry. Instead, we have our own artistic heroes who have brought new styles and perspectives to storytelling and art, including such genius figures as Lynda Barry and Alison Bechdel.

Perhaps the biggest lesson of cartoon school was the message of love and acceptance. Quite simply: they believed in us, and insisted that we should believe in ourselves because everyone has something to offer comics. Even those like me, who said "I absolutely cannot draw," were still encouraged to believe that we had something worthwhile to contribute, that brilliance was not about what you are born with but what you do, how you aim to transform. Sometimes getting there involves "feeling your fantasy": believing, or even insisting beyond the bounds of the realistic that you can do something, that you belong, that you can actually make things happen. You have to be bold to dive into the unknown and complete something. You have to imagine it being possible to risk your all for it.

I was working on my first comic about Sylvia Rivera when I decided to try a cat eye for the first time. I had been drawing the perfect arched brow, a big slick triangle of 1960s eye shadow, and a stacked lash on paper for weeks. I wrote the words "I am a drag queen!" over and over in word balloons. One day I decided to try it on myself. With black liquid eyeliner—like my cartoonist ink—I extended and obscured my eye shape into a messy hand-drawn slice of beauty.

Like comics, drag uses limited tools to create fantasy worlds out of our

"I LOOKED TERRIBLE."

imaginations. Drag is a multimedia creation, one that comes to life directly on the artist's body. Institutional art often needs lots of money and resources to make something, but drag and comics know how to innovate quickly and affordably, building community in accessible spaces—a bookstore, a bar, a makeshift stage. Artists from any background can be taken seriously in comics and drag. You don't need an expensive education or resources to make a mark.

After years of experimenting on the page, I could finally see the makings of a queen in me. I sketched myself on paper first then conjured the character from two dimensions onto my skin. Drag brought my art into three dimensions for the first time, and promised to propel me even further if I dared, throughout time and beyond space. Drag, like all art, lives on outside the artist, too, transformed by the audience.

Drag has become my favorite form of art, but I rarely see drag artists represented in the artistic canon. That is, at least, beyond a few busted pictures of Man Ray in old-lady drag or photos of Marcel Duchamp as the mysterious "Rrose Sélavy," or the like. The fact that these artists were straight is no coincidence; their drag is presented as art only on the condition that it is a metaphor for the nature of identity, not an authentic queer expression.

Barbette by Man Ray

Man Ray, however, was more familiar with queer expression than I might originally have thought. He photographed and befriended Barbette, the Texan drag aerialist who delighted Europe in the 1920s. The famously gay writer Jean Cocteau was obsessed with Barbette, and commissioned Man Ray to take photographs of her in various states of undress. Cocteau heralded the brilliance of drag, writing, "Thanks to Barbette, I understand that it was not merely for reasons of 'decency' that great nations and great civilizations gave women's roles to men." He saw that drag was a true art, motivated not by the exclusion of women, but a celebration that goes beyond gender.

Cocteau's favorite part of Barbette's act was the end, when she pulled of her wig and performed masculinity with as much artifice as she had the feminine. "The truth itself must be translated, if it is to convince us as forcibly as did the lie . . . The moment he has snatched off his wig, [he] plays the part of a man. He rolls his shoulders, stretches his hands, swells his muscles, parodies a golfer's sporty walk." Though Barbette enraptured audiences by the thousands, she is not remembered today as a brilliant artist the way Ray, Duchamp, and even Cocteau are. Despite decades of influence, drag's historical trailblazers are overlooked.

I bet the most expensive pieces of art depicting a person in drag are the self-portrait Polaroids of Andy Warhol in a tragic Marilyn look, at least one of which is owned by the Guggenheim Museum. I love Warhol's art—his screen print paintings are brilliantly designed and rendered. But his drag images are not very fabulous. By 1981, queens had long figured out how to cover their eyebrows, but judging from this photo, it seems no one wanted to help him with his. Perhaps this hints at how disconnected Warhol really was, despite his own queerness, from the queer scene he sometimes photographed. This is typical, too. When our artists gain mainstream recognition they are rarely celebrated for their connections to the larger queer community. Quite the opposite: a deep connection to queer culture may still be considered a disadvantage.

a Warhol-Style Polaroid

Reclaiming the great drag artists of history is something we must do for the world. Even if they did not care about being seen as important to the art world, representing them as such reminds everyone (including ourselves) that queer creativity is a universal and essential part of culture. We don't all gravitate to the same stories and figures from history, but we all must do our own kind of investigation into those who have come before us. Without understanding our context, we can never truly understand what needs to be done next. Of course, research on paper is not enough either. It wasn't until I became a queen myself, throwing out theory and just trying to do drag, that I really started to understand the fuller picture of our art form.

One of my first entry points to this history was reading RuPaul's first autobiography and researching the Wigstock Generation that surrounded her—the artists of the Pyramid Club and the Lower East Side of the 1980s and '90s. Many of these drag pioneers are still around to this day—upholding the traditions and continuing to make interesting and vital art. They saw drag as an exciting combination of artistic expression and political intervention that could be reinvented with every generation. Ru wrote, "The point about pop culture is that so much of it is borrowed. There's very little that's brand new. Instead, creativity today is a kind of shopping process—picking up on and sampling things from the world around you, things you grew up with." Reading her early words, and watching films like *Wigstock* and *Starrbooty* as well as the hours of raw footage by Nelson Sullivan recorded during that time and since uploaded to YouTube, I gained the utmost respect for RuPaul—an artist who hustled to make a name for herself, and continued to reinvent her approach until the world could truly see and hear her.

Leigh Bowery

It was this research that introduced me to Leigh Bowery, one of drag's most widely-respected artists. Leigh helped me see that my own drag would be better the more it broke all boundaries of traditional taste, beauty, and gender. Born in Australia, she was primarily known as the 1980s club promoter behind "Taboo," a London party that started as a gay underground phenomenon and became one of the city's most popular events. In the 1980s and '90s, Leigh traveled the world, debuting several fashion collections in London, New York, and Tokyo, performing at Wigstock, and more.

While London fashion designers like Zandra Rhodes and Vivienne Westwood had been mixing Regency silhouettes with punk symbols for years, and "scare" queens (like Divine) were common in clubs at the time, Leigh nevertheless broke the mold to lasting effect by taking every idea as far as possible, combining them with her own signature ornamentations and exaggerations. The impact of Leigh's fashion has only been further cemented since her death from AIDS in 1994. From the "Tranimal Drag" movement to haute couture runways and "club fashion" trends, Leigh's ideas, influence, and name live on.

Many of these references and histories have been passed down through an oral tradition, dished about after the gig, researched on social media, shared through scraps. It was from other queer artists that I first found out about and watched Moi Renee on YouTube, performing her song "Miss Honey" on New York City cable access TV in 1992. This mesmerizing clip has an energy and simple beauty that puts every video installation in a museum to shame.

Moi Renee

Other essentials included: Tandi Iman Dupree's legendary leap from the ceiling rafters into a split wearing a Wonder Woman costume while lip-syncing to "Holding Out for a Hero" at the Miss Gay Black America Pageant in 2001; Detox's lip-sync to Jefferson Starship's "Nothing's Gonna Stop Us Now"—the theme song from the camp movie classic *Mannequin*—where she freezes in a mannequin pose during the men's parts of the duet, holding an open purse for the audience to pour tips into; Raja's performance to Chaka Khan's "Through the Fire," where she shakes ashy powder out of her wig on every chorus; and Bianca Del Rio's performance at the *RuPaul's Drag Race* Season 6 premiere party, where instead of lip-syncing she cuts and sews a dress from scratch in only two minutes (I saw that one live!). I became particularly fascinated with a "Horror Lip-Sync Pageant" in the Philippines that featured a performance to "I Will Always Love You" where the queen interjects horrifying screams and monster moves. My mind was further blown by Sasha Colby's 2012 Miss Continental–winning performance, "Angels and Men," which to

Tandi Iman Dupree

this day remains one of the most dynamically executed drag routines I've ever seen. Getting to work with Miss Colby extensively through *NightGowns* was a dream come true.

Time and time again I saw drag and queer culture bringing brilliant and unforgettable ideas to our own simple, self-made platforms. I loved how drag performances could adapt to any setting: theaters and street corners alike. That's transformation—that's art!

Sasha Colby

In addition to these community legends, I saw some of the most brilliant art every day, around me, in my own local scene. I'll always remember when The Illustrious Pearl—who wrote poetry for the first issue of *Vym*—performed Dido's "White Flag" with a plastic bag tied to her ankle against a backdrop of the ocean. She explained that it was an allusion to the way immigrants sometimes have to tie their belongings in bags to swim across borders. Here, it told the story of the ongoing legal battle she was waging over her own undocumented status. At the end she pulled a white flag out of the bag and revealed it to be printed with a photo of her family.

The Illustrious Pearl

Another time I cried at a drag show was when transmasculine drag king Vigor Mortis performed "Mad World" and lip-synced "the dreams in which I'm dying are the best I've ever had" while he stripped out of a pink dress to reveal the word *boy* painted on his chest. The most brilliant artists were all around.

I could see firsthand that the art of drag wasn't limited to what was most visible in any scene or in any given time period. There is groundbreaking work all over. Our art, as a whole, is so much more than any of us knows, and that, perhaps most of all, gives me joy.

Vigor Mortis

When my mom died, I turned to drag because I needed to make something. I needed a project to work on, so I threw myself into it. Making new work helped me learn to store the grief over my mom's death somewhere safely, but also how to distract myself with laughter, metaphor, and a little beauty. Of course, grief can inspire art, but it can also get in its way. You've probably heard something along the lines of "art helps you process your pain and turn it into power." It's true, but not foolproof. What if the pain never goes away and the power never comes? It happens all the time. Fears and hurt can motivate, but they can never take you all the way. Transformation needs balancing forces.

I called my mother on her sixty-fourth birthday, a few days before she died, and she already sounded so tired. My dad said that call was the most she'd spoken all day. I flew back home the next morning. She couldn't speak by the time I arrived at the hospital in Illinois. Still, she was moving a lot—whispering to herself, occasionally breaking into a smile so big she looked like the Cheshire cat, and she, too, was fading away.

My dad slept at the hospital but I went home and plunked a few melancholy notes on the tiny piano I hadn't touched in six years. The only sheet music in the house was from *Titanic*, "My Heart Will Go On." She would have hated how sappy the scene was—she loathed sappy music. When I woke up the next morning she was dead.

When I got to the hospital, her body looked so much more like herself than she had when she was dying the night before, it was almost a relief to see. They removed her eyes in front of us; she decided to donate her organs—the few that didn't have cancer in them. Though the process was ghastly, it made me happy, because she wanted to give everything she had to those who needed it.

She was cremated later that week. A lady with purple lipstick and statement glasses who worked at the funeral home made me laugh that afternoon, describing her own fantasy funeral: thirteen crows released at midnight and a black coffin lined in black silk. Fabulous. We went in a more simple direction for my mother, though, respecting her wishes that we spread her ashes in the crashing waves of Land's End in San Francisco, where the ashes of my father's parents were also scattered.

On the day we did it, the flowers and vines were in bloom. I had hiked that same path with her many times, but the last time we were there, everything was dead and dried up from the droughts. I remember it made her cry.

I thought she was being a bit camp at the time, but seeing the rebirth of the chartreuse leaves and small yellow and pink blooms brought tears to my eyes the day we released her ashes into the Pacific Ocean.

Some people reached out when they heard; most didn't. I didn't take it personally. I learned that people are all support-ive in their own ways, some concerned with over-inserting themselves, others unsure how to help. Many of the people who did reach out were looking for reasons to talk about their own grief; mine was simply a mirror for theirs.

Communication brought up messes of emotions, and many days I preferred to avoid it altogether and work silently alone. I indulged in loneliness some days, and when I connected with people, I tried to use humor, storytelling, and exag-geration in addition to some brutal honesty. One of the biggest lessons we learn in drag isn't just how to change yourself, but how to celebrate the truths that cannot be changed, and make room for them.

My first night back in New York, I invited my friends Iru, Kelsey, and April over and we ended up watching a horror movie where an aging mom gets pos-sessed by a demon. The satanic woman runs around emaciated, with stringy hair, in a soiled nightgown, screaming and vomiting bile. It was a little exagger-ated and overstylized, but overall, she looked exactly the way my mom did on her deathbed. You'd think it would have been the wrong choice for the evening, but it was actually perfect. It was gory and real and camp and heartbreaking and

Land's End, 2015

funny and everything at once. A dying body is fucking scary and I needed to face it—to accept that life is full of horror and ridiculousness all at once, and to learn to love these as part of the whole deal.

I quit my day jobs to try being a full-time artist. I did a lot of website designs, some logos, and a few show posters. I said "yes" to every drag gig that came my way, even though I never made more than a hundred dollars. My dad helped me out by giving me my mom's life insurance—a total of twenty thousand dollars, paid in small monthly installments—so I could focus on making art and doing drag. We called it "The Jane Hedges Memorial Art Scholarship."

I developed a clear image of myself: stepping forward like a glamorous immortal witch, a mother of her community. Kind but piercing eyes, snatched face, strong shoulders, a curvaceous body, a fat ass, a corset, a black velvet gown, dangly earrings, and bright red glittering lips . . . just try to describe me without using the word *statuesque*! Through an influx of emotion, all the threads of my life, all

Posters I designed, 2015–17

my inspirations—grandmas, my mother, art, history, past drag performances, my community—combined and began to take shape as my own style of art, perhaps for the first time.

My mother was an amazing editor—she taught me how to revise my messages and designs to help everyone look and sound their best. She taught me how to edit, using a signature red pencil to leave questions, underlines, and circles on every kind of text. Sometimes you need to suggest a reword or restructure, take up a seam do a little shaping, contouring, highlighting. It's all about making the truth pop through all the words and forms. Editing is a form of art, too.

So I taught myself to revise, rehearse, and edit my drag. I photoshopped my drag photos and then made changes to my makeup and padding to match it in

real life. I wrote notes for my speeches, practiced them out loud in an empty room, and made more changes.

Before my mom passed, I was afraid of making bad art. I was so concerned with being too basic or too pretentious that I could never finish anything. After, I understood that I had nothing to lose, so I went ahead and tried. I started taking risks I wouldn't have dared if my mom had been alive. I wasn't afraid to embarrass myself. I realized I had been hiding some of my full heart and imagination still, worried what others think, and now I felt nothing holding me back from finally letting it all out, however many attempts it took.

I had an artistic breakthrough with my second gallery show, exhibited in the dark basement underneath Bizarre. I called the art series "Night Rooms" because it featured different digital prints, all depicting mysterious happenings taking place in nine different rooms. (And to sound like *NightGowns* in an act of dual promotion.)

A woman in mourning gazing out a pink baroque window. A detective watching a pigeon while smoking cigarettes in the bathtub. A terrified painter in a red room. The images looked like my monthly posters for the show but traced a loose narrative, a comic: glowing cubes of art that left a trail of bodies in their wakes, blurring together the old romantics and abstract modernists in explosions of primary and secondary colors.

When I look at the Night Rooms pieces today, I always think about Cas, aka drag king Vigor Mortis, who helped me hang each piece in Ikea frames on the basement walls. We spent hours drinking whiskey and talking about everything—from gender to religion, performance art to french fries. We discussed how it seemed like most successful artists had trust funds, and how we both had turned to studio art as a way of exploring our gender and queerness before we could identify them in ourselves.

166 ↖ "Night Rooms", 2016

My creative work—the comics, illustrations, sketches, essays—had all been a sketch of gender fluidity that I wanted to realize in myself. After I found that queerness in my real life, like Vigor, I realized my art didn't have the same therapeutic urgency as it did before. Now, it could move outward, creating a space for others to have those same realizations.

me & Cas/Vigor M.

In some ways, this breakthrough wasn't about the work at all, it was about the audience. Art comes to life by being seen. I loved watching and listening in real time to how the audience gave new meaning to the work. When the crowd of regulars filed down the basement stairs to check out my gallery, they made the work important, even if just for a second, by interpreting each piece through their unique sets of references. Artists should leave space for the audience to make the work about themselves, to use it as inspiration in their own future creations, or to just have a fabulous night.

Friends at "Night Rooms"

Onstage at the third *NightGowns* show, I finally put my thoughts into words. "I have learned that you must be honest about your pain, because you can—and must—think of it as something beautiful and yours," I began. "I learned that we do not ever lose these relationships—they just move inside. My mom exists inside my mind, among memories and fantasies—and that space in there is just as important, as real, as the one out here."

I had never before put personal stories from my life into my art, but now I found myself wanting, maybe needing to do so. It was okay to cry at the drag show, or so the audience started to tell me that night! By telling personal stories, but with surprising twists, I was able to connect with the audience on an even deeper level, unlocking new strengths and vulnerabilities in all of us. At the next *NightGowns* I put on one of my mom's eighties power suits and lip-synced to songs she had specifically told me she thought were too sappy. I didn't want to think in a simple binary anymore. "Good" and "bad" didn't really matter as long as it touched the audience, as long as it helped me stay in motion.

The distinction between good and bad, failed or successful art seems to have less and less of a clear meaning the older I get and the more experience I gain. Instead, what matters to me now is how people respond to my work, how it transforms them, and how that in turn changes me. I tried to put myself out into the world as the kind of queer superhero I had been drawing from the beginning. But "Sasha Velour" is an ongoing project, a transformation that goes on and on, reaching beyond my own limits and working to build connections through every genre, every medium, every possible way to reach people. To reach you!

Key

I spoke with ghosts to write this book. Or at least I really tried to. I burned sage and asked for clarity, then closed my eyes and did spirit drawings: it only yielded confused scribbles and the phrase "help me" in bubble letters. I pulled out the Ouija board: nothing but Z-A-Z-A (the sign of a demon, I later learned). I tried to let messages from the stars wash over me in the form of a playlist set to autoplay: cut to me listening to Shirley Bassey for three hours . . .

I struggled with writer's block and I'd lie on the floor imagining that my grandmas and drag legends alike were talking to me, telling me what they liked and didn't like, where I needed to state something clearer or make a different word choice.

In reality there are no quick fixes when it comes to making your best work. It doesn't hurt to try to channel other voices to help clarify your thoughts (even if those voices are found in your own imagination). But in the end, the voices inside us often only confirm what we already believe. You need real people, real community, real distance to balance out your own assumptions and superstitions.

If you want to reveal something new, you always have to do some investigation, finding the missing truths and making new sense of what you find. Great gestures don't come easy. In writing, it's just like being onstage—improvisation can be thrilling, but a little rehearsal, a lot of revision, and some well-timed reveals are a must!

My family taught me the importance of research and revision: Grandma Jo was a librarian who showed me how to check out books and use the card catalogs, my dad brought me to archives as his "research assistant" to make photocopies, and my mom, an editor and translator, taught me to take projects one step at a time, making clear lists of priorities. In her purse, she always kept a little notebook with running lists and reminders on it and added things in different sections whenever they came to mind. My mom's favorite advice for tackling anxiety: "Just set your intentions for the next hour, even the next fifteen minutes, and focus on that."

At the end of 2020, Johnny and I agreed to help my dad clean out the house

w/ My Dad & Daniela

in Illinois to get it ready for sale. He was just about to retire and was spending the winter in northern Italy to be with his amazing second-chance love, Daniela. I hoped that returning to my roots would help the creative process for this book. My dad left the key under the mat, and we dove in. We started by sorting through the endless boxes my mom had stored in our moldy basement, Vanya growling and barking at the mess.

My mom left many binders with paperwork and instructions on how to handle the legal issues surrounding her death. She kept a legend to the filing cabinet system, lists with contents of different boxes, and several binders with descriptions of how to run operations at the various jobs she held. She didn't finish everything, but she went out organized. I hope she was at peace with the unfinishability of her plans before she passed. Why waste a second of our unpredictable lives trying to be perfect or complete? But some days I couldn't help but feel like she was haunting us with her unfinished to-dos.

We gardened, cleaned out the old garbage, rearranged furniture, and tried to consolidate the family archives into boxes we could bring back to Brooklyn. But there was just so much. The house was flooded with photos, bank statements, train stubs, diaries, and letters. Vanya, for his part, stopped barking and jumped onto my mom's old armchair to curl up away from the piles.

As it turns out, my mother was a bit of a memory hoarder. Not only did she keep her priceless family treasures—vintage quilts and plates and linens—she kept tax documents, every piece of wrapping paper or gift box she'd received (flattened out in careful order), and every greeting card along with it. There was dry pasta art, and not just mine—I found some of her's from the 1950s! She had kept more of my art and school assignments than I could have imagined, including my blueprints circa age five for a city called "Howardville" (after my grandfather), which was disturbingly centered around a police station and a prison (they get into your mind early!).

There were also quite a few apology notes I had written between the ages of six and twelve. I found one I'd probably written around age nine that was so clear and earnest it made me laugh and cry at the same time:

"I'm so sorry for being so horrible. I hope you can forgive me. I don't see any reason to keep talking about it unless it is about how I can stop being so horrible. Love, Sasha." Maybe these discoveries really did help me understand myself better. Some days I still felt like that little kid, convinced I was doing things wrong, but desperately wishing I could avoid facing the consequences. Maybe I could try to be my own parent now and tell myself what I wished my mom and dad had said: "Nobody's perfect and nothing is that serious."

My drag sister Sasha Colby called me while I was in Illinois with a message from a psychic. "He asked me if I knew another Sasha in the Midwest and I immediately thought of you." I prepared myself for it. She went on: "I figured it was your mom coming through, and she wanted you to know that she understands why you were so busy while she was sick, you had to work. You don't need to worry. She understands." I smiled. I don't particularly believe psychics are real, but in a way it was oddly typical of my mom to "forgive" me for something I didn't know I needed to feel badly about. Bringing me a message through someone else seemed like my mom, too. She would always call my friends' houses to find me if I hadn't checked in on schedule.

I felt a wave of gratitude for the people in my life. There are so many ways to show your love—checking in, showing up, writing a love letter, keeping an archive, or just remembering. Who cares if ghosts aren't real? Our ideas of them help connect us to each other (or ourselves). Sometimes, a simple ghost story helps express truths that elude observation, something we know is lurking in the shadows . . .

Photos and scrapbooks can be kinds of ghosts, too. Sometimes all we have is a fragment, inspiring new questions to fill in the pieces, but also revealing possibilities we hadn't thought about. I learned so many new things about my

Dec 25 1996

Dear Mommy,

I'm sorry that I am being mean to you but I'm having a hard time and no one seems to care.

love,
Sasha

"apology" note

mom and dad by looking through their archives. I could finally see them fully as people—imperfect, human, childish—but that made me love and appreciate them even more. Although they had often tried to present themselves as authorities (that's kind of the whole gig of parenting), their archives revealed sweet and sensitive young people who were still learning, making mistakes, and changing their minds. I was able to watch the ways they had changed through the years—matured, refined, edited themselves.

My mom kept an archive of her own life in the form of scrapbooks, some of which I'd never seen. Newspaper clippings from 1968 when her Girl Scout troop sold enough cookies to take a monthlong trip to Europe; photos of her as a ballet dancer, slides of mountains and flowers from her time teaching English in Germany and Mexico in the 1970s; a diary entry where she describes running out of money and writing to her mom for help.

I found my dad's papers, too—a red leather travel journal from his 1974 student trip to China, a couple of photos from his San Francisco beads-and-protest days, and boxes upon boxes of microfiche primary source material about the Russian Revolution. He has always been interested in the same things, and wrote about everything with the drama of an epic storyteller. I found my dad's first love letters to my mom, where he dramatically described their different religious upbringings and cultures, praised her intellect, and dreamed of their future.

My mom, 1969 -

HAPPY ♡ DAY - MY GIFT FROM GREG & BARB

excerpt from
my Parents'
scrapbooks

my dad, 1974 ?

My parents let me choose which religious denomination I liked best. Following their own religious traditions, my mom took me to Presbyterian and Episcopalian Sunday services and my dad led the journey to Reform and Conservative Jewish congregations for Shabbat. In the end I chose Reform Judaism, drawn to the idea of eating ritual meals as a form of prayer. For years I studied Jewish history and Hebrew language after school and on the weekends. I was bar mitzvahed at thirteen and even taught Sunday school when I was in high school, reenacting Jewish fables with puppets that I made myself.

Of all the Jewish texts, I've always been most fascinated by the Talmud—a kind of "reading guide" to the Tanakh (or Torah) that contains many different interpretations of the text from different sources. It's a document that asks the reader to continuously revisit what they have read, and it embodies that visually on the page by using the margins to hold many disagreeing voices. According to Talmudic thought, in order to find the truth, we must be able to hold multiple possible meanings as true at the same time. That's the kind of book I always liked best—a scrapbook that brought many things together in conversation. It's so much more honest to reveal the amount of disagreement in life, our own biases as authors and readers. No one should mistake any points of view for definitive truths. Truth is found in the piecing-together.

I felt vindicated to learn that my legal last name, Steinberg, is a fake name, too. My great-great-grandfather came to the US from somewhere in the Russian Empire in the 1890s. It's believed he was escaping justice for some crimes he had committed with his uncles (family lore says it might have been murder). He didn't speak any English when he left for New York, but he saw the name Steinberg & Sons written on the side of a warehouse and recognized it as a "rich" Jewish name (like the names of wealthier Jews in Germany at the time) so he adopted it as his own upon landing on Ellis Island. We probably won't ever know our original name. For all we know it could have sounded closer to Velour.

My Jewish ancestors brought only a few pieces of silver and lace with them around the world. They had to tell (or make up) stories to remember who they were and where they came from. My mom's family, by contrast, preserved their family through artifacts: linens, quilting squares, cameo brooches, family trees, and evening gloves. The Taylors first came to America from Scotland in the 1500s, and moved west with each generation, slowly ending up in California by the time my mom was a little girl. While it's certainly a privilege to move freely, they didn't exactly live lavish lives. Mostly farmers and ministers, they held on to things mainly to reuse them: they salvaged old scraps of fabric to make new quilts, painted wooden chairs to freshen them up for the next generation, and passed down every teacup like a priceless treasure (I now have an unmatched set of ten cups and saucers).

Pieced together out of family quilts...

Quilts contain information about the people who made them, just like a story. A signature pattern, a shape, a favorite color, a personal embroidery can all reveal something about the maker. My mother sometimes pulled out the boxes of quilts, knitted blankets, and embroidered napkins, some dating back to the early 1800s made by relatives with names like "Pink" and "Minnie." She was never afraid to go in with scissors and transform something old into something new, recycling it into a new bag or a pillowcase. "It's better to enjoy it than keep it in a box" was one of her favorite mottos.

I suppose that's a metaphor for life! Every one of us is a working document, a quilt being completed and then repurposed all over again. We are made of different scraps, different stories and influences. While we are trying to become ourselves, we always end up discovering, reconsidering, discarding, and transforming a few pieces along the way.

My mom loved quilting. She would mix and match scraps from many clashing sources: centuries-old textiles from Kansas mixed with scraps she'd picked up on her travels. She loved tiny patterns, jewel tones, bright-colored prints, and triangles. The walls, televisions, beds, pillows, and chairs in our house were slowly covered in her abstract quilt art. I loved observing the process of quilting. Once the decorative pieces were sewn together, you have to stuff the blanket with batting and sew the backing onto the front with a new stitch pattern that goes through both sides, which creates yet another pattern on the finished blanket through thread alone. This was traditionally done as communal activity, because the work was too large for just one person. Like with all great projects, the company and help of others makes the final result better. And the celebration afterward? Divine.

There are so many different ways to remember. My dad's family told stories with punch lines and conclusions. My mother's family passed their history down with folk art. My drag family, my queer family, needed to be researched, sketched, and performed back into history.

In my drag family alone there are many family stories as diasporic and dramatic as mine. My chosen family has roots that crisscross the world in every different direction. I know Peruvian and Italian Americans who also had family in the New York garment industry; first-generation Chinese Americans who speak multiple languages; second-generation Filipino Americans with parents from different classes; Hawaiians with trans family histories going back generations.

But not all ancestry is so easily accessible. Too many records were banned or erased. Black Americans whose relatives were enslaved were denied official documentation, separated from family, and robbed of their language and cultures. To be cut off from the past can be violent, and we must help each other find the threads and put things back together.

The past can and must be revealed all around us. It's not a static, dead thing; the past is alive and well, shaping and being shaped by our current reality, whether we recognize it or not. Rewriting myths to recenter the erased Black, Indigenous, disabled, queer, and trans stories isn't an easy task. But art—including drag—helps fill in some missing pieces. Art can help us bring in new voices and perspectives from the past—not just with facts, but with realness and fantasy, too. Only when we have an understanding of our collective past can we truly live each day intentionally, and shape new ways forward.

Queer history is ever-evolving. New discoveries are made every day about where we came from. It's our job to rescue these heroes from obscurity and argue for their importance on the world stage. That's what happened in 2015, when writer and historian Channing Joseph shared new research about William Dorsey Swann, the formerly enslaved nineteenth-century queer activist, who was later dubbed "America's First Drag Queen." Swann's history of resistance against the criminalization of homosexuality and drag was a revolutionary discovery. Despite having only a few pieces of her incomplete story, queer people responded to the news immediately, and her legacy quickly became part of the evergrowing drag canon.

In a case of new myths replacing old ones, a photo of "William Dorsey Swann" was circulated first by *The Nation* in 2020, but I learned while researching this book that it was a photo of a totally different person!

Jack Brown

There are no known photos of the real Swann. There are photos that depict Jack Brown, a famous vaudeville drag performer who helped popularize the dance called the "cakewalk" at the turn of the twentieth century. This particular photo comes from a series that Brown took in Paris in 1903.

My dad was the first to send me photos of a similar drag story from St. Petersburg, Russia, that had recently been unearthed. In 1921, a St. Petersburg (then called Petrograd) drag ball was busted by the police, exposing navy sailors, artists, and businessmen alike dressed in drag looks of the latest fashion, along with drag kings in suits. At the time, many knew about the German drag scene, and looked to then famous stars like Hansi Sturm of Berlin's

"Red wedding" 1921

Eldorado Club for inspiration. Unfortunately, the organizer of the so-called Red Wedding party, a sailor named Afanasy Shnaur, betrayed his own community and reported them all to the secret police. They were arrested but the charges didn't stick (that era of early socialism was more progressive than Russia today).

Drag is always illuminating new connections and challenging our established sense of history. I continued to learn new stories and encounter icons I hadn't met before in the final stages of putting this book together.

I was particularly grateful to connect with Marlow La Fantastique, a stunning trans performer who held the copyright to a photo of Crystal LaBeija that I wanted to use. I learned Marlow had herself been a finalist in the same 1967 Miss All-America Camp Beauty Pageant (she's even in a publicity photo from "The Queen" right next to Crystal), and later worked as a star of Finocchio's, and in the Berlin cabaret scene. Queer history is full of surprises, revealing new stories and complexities with every turn. I love the chaos! Like the philosopher Walter Benjamin said, nothing that has ever happened and been forgotten should be regarded as lost to history. The past, like the present, is a moment waiting to be found, ready to be transformed by the future.

Marlow La Fantastique & Crystal La Beija

If we want to be seen as legendary, we have to weave ourselves into history. If I were to make a quilt of drag, I'd want pieces from all over. A stretched hide from a shaman's tent; silk from Gladys Bentley's tuxedo; sequins from Divine's wiggle dress; hair from RuPaul's wig.

Each of us is just a small fragment of a larger picture, whether we admit it or not. Today there are many famous drag performers, but it's not the first time queer art has been visible. Throughout the nineteenth and twentieth centuries, Du Val, Vesta Tilley, Barbette, Mei Lan-Fang, and more all grew to be world famous. But today many people, even drag queens, haven't heard their names. Even fewer know of Coccinelle, Kewpie, or Akihiro Miwa despite the impact on their communities, and their undeniable artistry! Do we as queer people have the privilege to be seen as part of a real cultural legacy and tradition, or will we continue to be written off as a flash in the pan, a joke, just for fun?

It is a privilege to have context and history, one drag has rarely been given. Let's arm ourselves with information about where we come from—the injustices and the spirit of resistance. Even after we tell our histories, we will need to research, edit, tell, and revise it again, so that it feels relevant and vital to each generation. We want to challenge our old myths, not write and enforce new ones.

Before I was Sasha Velour, I was always Sasha. Even though my legal name is Alexander, my family called me Sasha from before I was born. My parents named me after philosopher Alexander Herzen and feminist revolutionary Alexandra Kollontai, both Russian progressives from history whom they felt strong connections to. If they hadn't spotted a little something extra between my legs on the ultrasound, they apparently would have chosen "Esther" (the heroine of the Purim myth) as my name, which was at least one reason I was very happy to have been born a "boy." I always loved my name, but I had never met another Sasha who wasn't an old Russian man until the early 2000s, when I read that Beyoncé "is gripped by a spirit so powerful, it even had a name: Sasha!" I almost passed out.

I cut those words right out of the *Rolling Stone* and added them to my inspiration wall—a wannabe dadaist collage made out of garbage behind my closet door. Her pull quote became one of the central pieces forming a constellation with a Russian icon wrapped in birch, a pink triangle gay pride sticker from a local student interest fair, a theater stub from *Phantom of the Opera*, and a photo of the cast of the original *Queer Eye*. "Yes, the rumors are true," I'd tell an imaginary audience, gesturing feyishly to my wall art. "Beyoncé says she channels *me* onstage!" I found this collage intact when cleaning my dad's house. I took a picture, then removed it piece by piece, saving the Beyoncé scrap to put in my new "Diva Shrine"—right next to a piece of Lady Gaga's costume that fell off when she visited the set of *Drag Race*!

Beyoncé in Rolling Stone, 2004 →

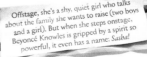
Offstage, she's a shy, quiet girl who talks about the family she wants to raise (two boys and a girl). But when she steps onstage, Beyoncé Knowles is gripped by a spirit so powerful, it even has a name: *Sasha!*

Of course, Beyoncé killed off her Sasha stage persona a decade later, saying she learned she didn't need to hide her real self in order to experiment with her image. I feel the same way: I don't need a drag name. Sasha Velour is my real name now. This is who I really am, and always have been, no transformation needed.

Drag is a job that has allowed me to own and find fulfillment in authentic parts of myself: my femme strength and my nonbinary creativity. I call myself gender fluid, which means that whether I'm in full feminine eveningwear, masculine sportswear, a butch tuxedo, or anything in between, I feel like it's an authentic extension of myself. I'll wear dresses, heels, jewelry, even makeup when not onstage, for my own enjoyment. Plus, who's to say a dress can't be masculine? Or that a hiking boot can't be femme? Gender comes together in the styling, the way you piece things together and wear them. Coming to understand myself as gender fluid has changed how I view drag. I don't think my drag needs to be traditionally feminine. Instead, I see it as an exaggeration of my entire gender fluidity, the entire me. There's no "real me" to reveal underneath the drag—the final reveal is a full, kaleidoscopic presentation of my real self—and all it can be—lit up and celebrated, actualized through my drag.

"Sasha Velour" was made like a quilt. I took pieces of who I had been, where I came from, and what I had seen and pieced them into something new, using the stitching techniques my mom taught me, filling in gaps and holes with stories of my own that seemed to match. I came up with my own pattern to tie all the chapters, constellations, and stories together, adding signature flourishes and shapes to make it into something new. Best of all, it took community to finish me up, weave me together, see me as whole, and push me out into the world: a quilt, a collage! A book!

And what's next? For me, it's not so much a question of whether drag will remain at the cutting edge of culture (it will), but of what fantasies and nightmares it will bring along the way. I predict drag will grow more inclusive, more expressive, more successful. But as it becomes more widespread, it might also become more ill-informed, more politically divided, more detached from its full potential. Progress is cyclical, and it falls to individuals to stand up for the truth in changing times.

I wrote this book to give a little record of one more queer person . . . I lived, I loved, I was here—mess and all. I wrote this book to prove without a doubt that drag is natural and can disrupt boundaries of masculine and feminine, self and community, art and revolution, past and present, success and failure. Drag belongs on the world stage, like queer people belong in the world!

Now I'm passing this archive on to you. If you are reading this, you're part of my family now—who else would want to read these stories? I hope you can use this book in your own life: as a tool to show how drag can be revolution, camp, and art at the same time; as a textbook to learn the queer histories of religion, drama, and costume; at least as a prop for your bookshelf. I suggest using it as a fortune-telling deck—choose a page at random, then channel the image or phrase you land on for the day.

I need to warn you: please don't take anything I have written too seriously. I have learned many wonderful things from my ancestors, but I also had to find my own points of agreement and disagreement, transforming every piece I was given into something that worked for me. You shouldn't just accept and internalize what you're being told. Life demands that you interpret it and make something new.

Last but not least, as my family: please know that upon my death I would like to be cremated and put into the ocean with the rest of my family. All of my dead relatives' ashes have been illegally dumped into oceans and lakes, since no one was wealthy or religious enough for a grave. They all loved traveling so much, and I hope to join them in motion in the water.

Or you know what . . . even more decadently: maybe you could turn my ashes into a giant fuchsia diamond and toss me into the ocean like the old lady at the end of *Titanic*! Yes . . . I love that. Nothing wrong with adding a little unnecessary glamour and tackiness to old tradition. Watch as my fuchsia facets crash into the waves with a *Splash!*

[Cue music]

★ SPLASH!

I love the chaos of growth!
MMMM SO FRESH!
Where are you, Grandma?

We need to ask you for a favor, Grandma!
I'm digging around in the back, darling!
Just a second, my darling! I could get really lost in here...

Grandma! It's an artistic EMERGENCY!

That one was from years ago!

The same year that Grandma performed at the Folies Bergères!

What is that again? An old strip club?

AWWWWW...

Ancient history, babe! I'm touched that you remember...

Well...you've told the story so many times...

Kiss!

Let's see how it looks, my darlings!

THIS!!! I love it!

WOW!
Revolutionary! Groundbreaking! ...SO camp!
Work! That costume actually looks good on you! The drama!
I feel like a powerful queen!
That's the shot! Give me ART...
As much as I hate to miss this, I have to go grab the veggies before the storm comes...
Go ahead, love! I'll stay and watch this little ritual!

YES BEAUTIES!
I'm so proud of you kids. All I could have dreamed of was a world where you could be yourselves. Like this...natural, free!
...and where you could make me feel like my most treasured costumes are terribly dated!
ha ha ha!
Not that I'm dying or anything. Grandma will live forever, and she'll haunt you after she dies... giving you a little tickle here, a surprise there! At least, that's what I was raised to do!
I LOVE IT!!
But if I were going... I'd want to remember this moment.

3,2,1...
Grandma is talking about dying again! Don't think we can't hear you!
But since you mention it...can I have the house?
LOVE
gorgeous!
I'm glad you didn't get rid of this outfit, Grandma!
I never get rid of clothes! You can always transform them into something else...
*Click
That's so old school. I love it!

And I mustn't forget to do something about this little book!
Oh, What a world...
Oh...hello there, you good little kitty!
I didn't see you! Come on inside...
MEOW
There's no place like home...
PURRR...

Acknowledgments

Big thank-you to my incredible editor, Jenny Xu, for seeing this project through from the beginning and helping me to quilt it together from fragments. I am also indebted to my many personal and creative heroes: Sylvia Rivera, RuPaul, Leslie Feinberg, Laurence Senelick, Linda Simpson, JD Doyle, José Esteban Muñoz, and closer to home—my dad, Papa Velour; Miss Malice; Lady Quesa'Dilla; Glace Chace; and so many others. To Johnny Velour and Vanya—thank you for keeping me insane and also holding me close. And last but not least, I am especially thankful to the incredible women in my family who gave me life and left too soon: my mom, Jane; and my grandmothers, Dina and Josephine.

Cover Design: Sasha Velour, Olivia McGiff

Cover Photographs (and opening spreads): Tanner Abel and Nicholas J. Needham

Endpapers: Johnny & Sasha Velour

Comics and Interior Art: Sasha Velour

Interior Layout: Nancy Singer

Chapter Portraits: Mettie Ostrowski

Instax: Nicole Lutz, Mettie Ostrowski and Johnny Velour

Comics Models (in order of appearance): Sasha Velour, Linda Simpson, Nicholas J. Needham, Mettie Ostrowski, Bronwyn Karl, Tanner Abel, Miss Malice, Miwa Sakulrat, Vigor Mortis, Neon Calypso, and Jenna Hanlon

Costuming and Wigs: Diego Montoya, Pierretta Viktori, Sergio Castaño Peña, Florence D'Lee, Casey Caldwell, Robert Sorrell, Diana Dash, Cristophe Mecca, Marco's Wigs, Wigs & Grace, Wing & Weft Gloves, Schiapparelli

IMAGE NOTES

All images are from the House of Velour unless otherwise credited.

2   Buryat *shaman*, early twentieth century. From The Library of Congress.

3   We'wha (a Zuni *lhamana*) weaving, on a trip as a cultural ambassador to Washington, DC, ca. 1886, John K. Hillers. From The Harry Ransom Center, The University of Texas at Austin.

3   Three *machi* of the Mapuche, 1900. Via Wikimedia Commons.

4   Cover of *Transgender Liberation: A Movement Whose Time Has Come* © 1992 Leslie Feinberg. Accessible in PDF at no cost at workers.org/book/transgender-liberation.

7   My grandparents Dina and Norman Steinberg (*standing*) with my grandparents Jo and Howard Hedges (*seated*), San Francisco, CA, 1980.

8   Grandma Dina's immigration card, 1939.

8   Grandma Dina, ca. 1949.

8   Cover of a *Finocchio's* souvenir program, ca. 1950. Courtesy of Queer Music Heritage.

8   Dressing up with Grandma Dina at her condo in Stockton, CA, 1995.

9   Dressed as a "Sorceress," 1995.

9   Grandma Jo, ca. 1931.

9   Dressed as "Cinderella," 1990.

10   British troops in drag for a Christmas charity performance, which was interrupted by an alert, Gravesend, England, 1940, John Topham. © TopFoto.

10   Grandma Jo's brother Clyde in "drag," 1981.

14   Clipping from *The Afro-American*, 1932. Courtesy of Queer Music Heritage.

14   Magnus Hirschfeld and friends dressed up for a party at the Institute, ca. 1920s. From the Magnus-Hirschfeld-Gesellschaft, Berlin.

15   Photo of Lynn Carter and Stormé DeLarverie from a *Jewel Box Revue* program, early 1960s. Courtesy of Queer Music Heritage.

15   Poster for a Newark engagement of the touring *Jewel Box Revue*, ca. 1967. Courtesy of Queer Music Heritage.

15   Promotional Ashtray from Mona's, early 1950s. Courtesy of Queer Music Heritage.

16   Painting of Barbette, 1926, Charles Gesmar. Via Wikimedia Commons.

16   Barbette, ca. 1920s, Wilhelm Willinger. Courtesy of the Theatre Museum, Vienna.

17   Poster for an appearance of Danny LaRue on the West End, Electric Modern Printing Company LTD, 1973. From the Prince of Wales Theatre (Delfont Mackintosh Theatres).

17   Members of the Gay Liberation Front, demonstrating outside Bow Street Court, 1971. © PA Images/Alamy.

18   Sylvia Rivera in front of her home on Pier 45, New York, NY, 1996, Valerie Shaff. From Valerie Shaff.

18   Kewpie in drag at the Marie Antoinette Ball

♡♡♡♡♡

Special thanks to the thousands of artists across the world who have given me beautiful fan art over the years. Pieces from the following artists appear in this book:

Adrian Mar aka Choriza May

Amy Ackerman

Betty Whatsherface

Bijou Bentley

Carrie King

Chara Couture

Christian Abou Fayssal

Denise Quintanilla

Freya Almond-Palmer

Jeremy Sorese

Katie Duval

Kaylee Arama

Laurel Lynn Leake

Mauve

Nataliya Gurba

Raina Rue

Rodrigo Salazar

Yumi

♡ the end!

xo
SASHA

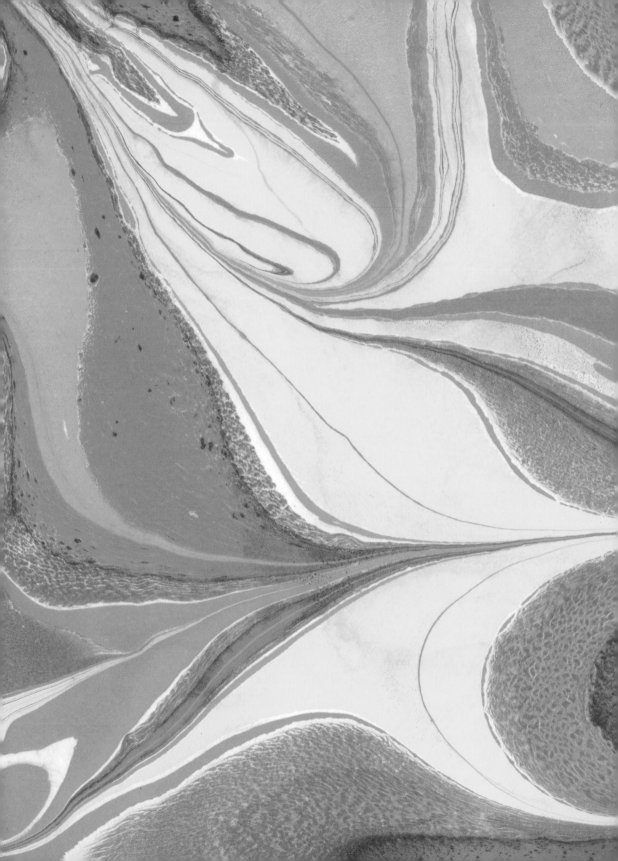